Zentrepreneurism

Allan Holender

THE BOOK TREE
San Diego, California

Zentrepreneurism – A 21st Century Guide to the New World of Business

Copyright © 2006, 2008 by Allan M. Holender

All rights reserved.

ISBN 978-1-58509- 114-0

UPDATED SECOND EDITION

Cover Layout: Toni Villalas
Cover design: Leon Phillips
Author Photo: Jaime Kowal
Editing: Paul Tice

Holender, Allan, 1941 –

   Zentrepreneurism : A 21st century guide to the new world of business /
   Allan Holender

1. Business – Religious aspects – Buddhism. 2. Entrepreneurship.

Printed in USA

 Published by
The Book Tree
P O Box 16476
San Diego, CA 92176
www.thebooktree.com
We provide fascinating and educational products to help awaken the public to new ideas and
information that would not be available otherwise.
Call 1 (800) 700-8733 for our *FREE BOOK TREE CATALOG*.

"We have a situation where we don't trust our government or our capitalist system and the level of distrust right now is probably unparalleled since the 1930s."

—Charles Lewis
Founder, Centre for Public Integrity

"People are expecting more from the companies they're working for and more from the companies they're doing business with and more from the companies they're buying from."

—Sydney Finkelstein
Professor of Strategy and Leadership
Dartmouth's Tuck School of Business

WORDS OF PRAISE FOR A GROUNDBREAKING BOOK

To manifest his vision, Allan has midwifed Zentrepreneurism—*to spark and serve a need to devlop ethics and spirituality within the mundane and sometimes dirty world of business. He cites many examples of leaders who have incorporated varying measures of ethics and spirit into their entrepreneurial organizations. Read the book, and take something of value from it.*
—Arran Stephens, founder & CEO of Nature's Path, North America's largest organic breakfast foods company

I'm delighted to be called a "zenner" and have been for quite a few years now. My company, Weapons of Mass Entertainment, has many entrepreneurial ventures in the works, all of which will impact the planet in a positive way. I hope many of you get the same buzz I got when reading Zentrepreneurism. *Life is too short to mess around doing other stuff... start zenning today!*
—Dave Stewart, President, Weapons of Mass Entertainment

The birth of Zentrepreneurism *is a new way of looking at business and the triple bottom line. The author believes the hope lies with the emergence of zentrepreneurs who create successful and purposeful businesses. From beginning to end a book I could not put down.*
 —David Litvak, Cascadia Publicity

Please thank Allan Holender for planting such a wonderful seed, and let him know the rest of us will work very hard to plant many more, so that before long we can all enjoy a senseful world. I'm very anxious to meet him, as I find him to be somewhat of a silent mentor for me. For me, I've been waiting a lifetime for these very important integrity-driven concepts to take hold. I've always lived within a strong sense of doing the right thing for myself and others. So, with all of my gratitude, thank you!
—Michael DeHaven, Zentrepreneur

Corporate America (and business the world over) is blessed that YOU are the one with the strength, conviction, passion and insight to lead us during such an otherwise unsettling and pivotal time. It is long overdue that the worlds of business, self-help and spirituality come together for not only the good of business but for the good of humanity.
—Michael Rosone, Managing Director, SoundBoard, New Jersey

Table of Contents

Dedication

This book is dedicated to:

- My son Daniel, whose courageous words and actions led me to find the real Allan Holender,
- My grandchildren Taylor and Mikayla, who bring hope for the future with their innocence and trust,
- My daughter Lisa and son-in-law Michael, for their patience and forgiveness,
- My life's companion Roxanne, who never gave up believing that I would some day realize my full potential,
- My late father, to whom I could never find the words to say the things I can now write about,
- My loving mother, who always believed her son was special.
- My philosophical mentor, the late Dr. Harold Tascher of the University of Montana,
- My life mentor, Jon-Lee Kootnekoff,
- My Zen mentor and friend Bruce Stewart, who inspired me to complete this book.

And to everyone I have met since my life journey began at conception and birth. I believe you were all brought into my life for a reason, and for that I am grateful and feel blessed. A special thanks to Arlene Prunkl, my editor, who took a special interest in my work and Leon Phillips who designed this exceptional cover and understood that it would serve as a gateway to the soul of a Zentrepreneur. And finally to the entire graduating class of the first course on Zentrepreneurism. When the teacher is ready, the students show up.

Foreword

by Bruce A. Stewart

Not every generation is privileged to see the start of a future. We are – and in *Zentrepreneurism*, Allan Holender has acted as its revelator, its prophet, if you will.

We are used to thinking of prophets as heralds of a far-off future. But prophets simply crystallize what is ready to be born: the world of social and natural capitalism, the world of full-life living, the world of service coupled with entrepreneurial behavior that this book describes, has been building for the past thirty years. Only now is it ready to shine forth in the full light of day.

With this revelation, the business world – and our personal lives – are destined to change. There is little question that many of us today are seeking something beyond what the world has offered us to date. Whether your life reflects great success in your endeavors, or whether each day is a personal or professional struggle, work alone isn't enough for many of us now. Instead, we are looking for a whole-life experience, one where all the pieces come together. Work becomes love, love becomes living, and living is work. We seek a life where our partners, our families, our businesses and our efforts merge into a single, harmonious whole – and where we measure our success in more ways than just the balance in our bank accounts.

Harmony requires as much from us as it gives us. We live harmoniously when our efforts lead to a more harmonious environment. Unsurprisingly, the pioneers who brought us simple messages about work/life balance and integration into a single whole have also pioneered humane environments that take as much care with the environment, with the community, and with the groups of many people as I could, and then synthesized my discoveries and experiences of these events in the book. I am a communicator, and so what better role to have as a first time author than to be the voice and messenger for Zentrepreneurism. I hope you can use this in your own life and business.

1

From Bar Mitzvah to Buddha

Dr. Graham Howe, one of Britain's top ranking psychiatrists, said:

> *"To read a little of Buddhism is to realize that the Buddhists knew, two thousand five hundred years ago, far more about our modern problems of psychology than they have been given credit for. They studied these problems long ago and found the answers also. We are now discovering the Ancient Wisdom of the East."*

The Buddha was the first to throw intelligent light on the human mental process. The important thing for us to remember is that the mind controls our speech and our actions, so the nature of the mind determines what we say and do. Because the Buddha taught his followers that they themselves make or mar their own happiness, so we must rely on our own efforts and not seek salvation from a deity or supernatural being. According to the teachings of the Buddha, if a man relies simply on himself, it is considered a weakness to seek aid and favors by praying. Instead of prayer, Buddha taught his students to meditate and develop the mind so we would be able to face life's difficulties and overcome them. In the process, we learn that neither suffering nor happiness is permanent. In the case of happiness, we only need a little patience and fortitude to wait for things to change.

This self reliance was a very difficult process for me to achieve. Since childhood I grew up with the belief that God would either protect or punish me. If I did good, he would protect me; if not, I would pay the ultimate retribution. In the Jewish belief system, there is one day when we must atone for all our sins of the year and that is the holiest of days, Yom Kippur.

On this day, we are told to confess all our sins, that we will be forgiven by God, and he will write us into the book of life for another year. If we don't admit our guilt, dire consequences will befall us. Until a Jewish boy has his bar mitzvah, his parents are responsible for all of his sins, but when he reaches the age of thirteen, he is considered to be entering manhood and therefore becomes totally accountable for himself. My mind boggles with all the things we got away with as kids. It is a rude awakening after the bar mitzvah speech, to begin immediately to be judged for everything you do. I immediately went home and hid my *Playboy* magazines. Because of an over reactive Mother, all things became catastrophic. My mother and I would engage in endless prayer sessions with every minor cold and scratch.

Another inherited trait with European Jews is "superstition." I was never allowed to say I was well or happy, because to do so would cause an *anhora*, an evil spell of some sort. If somebody asked me how I was and I replied I was doing "Great," my Mother would immediately invoke a protective clause by uttering the words "canahora poo poo poo." (roughly speaking), spitting three times. Hence one of the reasons why the majority of Jewish men are in therapy or are psychiatrists themselves.

The Buddhist is at a great advantage because he does not lose sight of reality during the happy moments and he does not give away to despair in the face of misfortune. The Buddhist knows that existence is controlled by balanced natural laws and prayer can only be used to express a desire that these laws should change for one's individual benefit, or that we wish for something we have not earned or are not entitled to. If natural laws could be upset in this way, we would be obtaining things at someone else's expense.

In almost every one of the great religions of the world, faith is required of the followers because many of the teachings and doctrines are incompatible with reason. Buddhism strikes a great contrast in this respect; the Buddha asked only for confidence based on understanding and reason. He taught that blind acceptance is of no use to an individual because it does not require enough depth of knowledge to make it valuable or serve as a guide along life's path. This broad outlook is one of the reasons Buddhism is now finding so many ready converts in the West.

Is this the true story of a Jew who became a Buddhist? Not really. I'm just a fellow traveler on the journey, seeking the same things you are. This, then, is my invitation for you to join me, as we open the door to Zentrepreneurism and a new world of doing business.

Buddha says:
"If one finds a friend with whom to fare, rapt in
the well-abiding rapt, surmounting dangers one
and all with joy, fare with him mindfully."

Embracing Compassion

Despite its wealth, the United States, has the smallest proportionate middle class and the greatest gap between rich and poor of any industrialized nation. As more and more Americans fall through the cracks into privation and poverty, they also fall victim to the predatory economic institutions that Howard Karger examines so thoroughly and powerfully in his book *Shortchanged*. Like such classics as *Nickel and Dimed*, *Shortchanged* is a wakeup call for action to redirect our economy toward fairness and ethics.

What is fundamentally right about the above statement and so dangerously wrong? Well, if we take a hard look at the underbelly of America we might not like what we see. A nation priding itself on being a land of great opportunity and wealth, and a land where immigrants came and staked their claim to the American dream. All things are possible in America: just start a business and you will achieve enormous wealth. That was the promise, an inviting scenario. Jim Jones said, "Drink the Kool-Aid and you'll reach Nirvana." Somebody lied!

I remember forty years ago when I graduated from the University of Montana, my Uncle Leon from Philadelphia asked me a direct question: Are you going to stay in the U.S. after graduation or go back to Canada? I said I hadn't made up my mind yet. His response was equally pointed. How could I possibly think of returning to Canada? I would not have the same opportunities to get rich as I would have in the good ol' USA. Also, Canada is so backward and America is blessed with so much more of everything. He left out the part about having more "poverty" in America than in Canada, and a health system in Canada that helps people get better as opposed to a system in the U.S. that enables the rich to get well and the poor to get sicker, and the middle class to go bankrupt. America the beautiful or America the tarnished? But hey, more incentive to make more money, right? Wrong. What price glory?

My uncle and his family and, for that matter, all my American relatives equated a high degree of success in life to the acquisition of personal wealth. Becoming a successful lawyer or doctor or owning a multimillion-dollar company with the accompanying "nice" Jewish girl and split-level mansion in the suburbs was the ultimate goal, and deserving of bragging rights to the rest of the family. And if you should have the misfortune of being a truck driver or shoe salesman, alas, much pity would befall your parents for producing such a social misfit.

It's the *Goodbye, Columbus* syndrome of Jewish dating, starring Richard Benjamin and Ali McGraw. A Jewish man and a Jewish woman meet and although they're attracted to one another, they find their worlds are very different. She is the archetypal Jewish American Princess, very emotionally involved with her parents' world and the world they have created for her. He, on the other hand, is much less dependent on his family. They begin an affair that brings more differences to the surface.

In the movie *Goodbye Columbus* Neil Klugman works in the public library and lives in New York with his Jewish aunt rather than in Arizona with his parents. College girl Brenda Patimkin very much lives with her well-to-do Jewish family. Even so, the two are attracted and start seeing one another. As the relationship gets more serious, Brenda's mother becomes increasingly hostile toward Neil, thinking her daughter will end up marrying beneath her.

There is a certain degree of logic and rationale to this syndrome. After all most Jewish immigrants who came to the United States had escaped the unspeakable horrors of the Nazis in concentration camps and they were holocaust survivors. My belief is that they wanted a life for their children that was totally opposite to what they had experienced. So they went overboard, wanting only the best of everything for their kids.

Also, there was a belief that the only way Jews could escape anti-Semitism was to work for themselves. I took that belief with me into society and became paranoid every time I had a gentile boss. Would he find out I was Jewish and then find a reason to fire me? The best decision I ever made was to leave Edmonton and attend an American college, the University of Montana, which then had a population on campus of three Jewish students and 3,200 gentiles. My first roommate was Tom Gillon from Chester, Montana, who had never heard of a Jew, and my second was George Paige, a black football player from Portland, whose father was a judge. When I tried out for the basketball team, I met Ray Lucien, the only black guy on the team. Ray was from Baton Rouge and his was a poverty stricken family. The only jacket Ray had was the letterman jacket he got for being on the team. He loved that jacket – even slept in it.

I have fond recollections of those days, which seemed remarkably free of prejudice. George, Ray, and I would often have dinner together talking about our futures. We took different paths, but I believe we had one thing in common: a genuine sense of compassion, trust, and love for another. At that time, I could not understand the resentment my relatives had for the blacks in South Philadelphia, viewing them as being no more than second-class citizens. I would ask them, "How can you persecute them, when we have been the persecuted ones from generation to generation?" Their answer was a subtle form of racism. *"You don't know how they live because you're not around them."*

I love my extended Philadelphia family, but I don't have to like their beliefs. The frightening part is that I honestly believe they represent much of mainstream white America's thinking. They moved three times from their South Philadelphia home, and each time it was to an all white suburban neighborhood. When Overbrook Park became inhabited by blacks, they moved to Overbrook Hills, and finally, to an all white gated retirement community in Florida.

I began to become less paranoid about being Jewish and more accepting of the equality in us all. Having grown up entirely in a protective "Jewish only" environment, I began to assimilate with the rest of the world, beginning my ascent into having "compassion" for all beings. Not an easy task for a "brain-washed" only child who believed everything his mother and father told him. This is not to say I did not experience my own share of bullying and anti-Semitism as a child. I did, but my dad, God bless him, always told me to not fight back – to simply walk away and feel sorry for the attackers. At that time, I became more passive than aggressive in the resolution of conflict, more judicious in my understanding of people, their motivation to become angry, and the price to pay for fighting and war.

Buddha says:
"To feel true compassion for all beings,
we must remove any partiality from
our attitude toward them."

Our normal view of others is dominated by fluctuating and discriminating emotions. We feel a sense of closeness toward loved ones, while with strangers or acquaintances we feel distant. For those individuals who we perceive as hostile, unfriendly, or aloof, we feel aversion or contempt.

The criterion for our classifying people as friends or enemies seems straightforward – if a person has caused us difficulty or harm, he or she is a foe. Mixed with our fondness for our loved ones are emotions that inspire passionate intimacy, such as attachment and desire. Similarly, we view those whom we dislike with negative emotions such as anger and hatred. Consequently, our compassion toward others is limited, partial, prejudicial, and conditioned by whether we feel close to them. Genuine compassion must be unconditional. Now I'm sure, if you are reading this on the New York subway, it's difficult to adopt this concept and attempt to view the stranger sitting next to you with compassion.

However, if we are to begin this journey toward enlightenment and follow the Eightfold Path of Buddha, compassion is high on the list. Once you become aware of this, your eyes will open to the way we are used to interacting with all beings. Sometimes in conversation I still catch myself only partially listening to responses. I'm already moving ahead with my own agenda. Now I pay particular attention to what people are saying, who they are, and what they have to say about their business and their lives. I have discovered you can connect with people at a deeper, more compassionate level, without becoming a therapist, and you can be free to just LISTEN!

As I scanned the room, I noticed how the "newbies" were squirming in their seats, while the converts were raising their hands and saying yes at the appropriate prompting of my friend, the leader. The standard sets of questions were asked, i.e., "How many of you want to have success and wealth in your lives? How many of you want to learn the seven secrets of the top millionaires in the world? How many of you are truly happy in your life now? How many of you would like to have a loving and successful relationship with your spouse or partner? How many of you would like residual income so that you can give to the charity of your choice? How many of you would like to live your life to the fullest? How many of you believe a million dollars is enough to retire on?" And for the closing, "If I could teach you the seven ways to achieve ultimate happiness in your life and your business, what would that be worth to you?"

I found I couldn't take much more. I was about to leave when mercifully he asked us to break into groups of three in order to exchange goal setting ideas. I bolted for the door. Out in the fresh air, I took a deep breath and thanked the universe for delivering me from the hype and glory seekers to a place of right action, right mindfulness, right livelihood, truth, integrity, and compassion. I make no apologies for the fact I am just learning the Buddha principles; I have found more joy in being a recent student on this path than I ever had in a lifetime of buying franchises, becoming a Multi-Level Marketing (MLM) distributor or running motivational self help workshops for fun and profit.

Think about it. What would you like to have written at your grave site or spoken at your eulogy? "Bob was a great guy, he had triple his sales quota in 2004, he drove a brand new Jaguar, had a 24,000 square foot house with a pool, he built a business empire and retired a multi-millionaire, he always measured his success by his wealth and building crucial skills in today's business world. He led effectively with cutting-edge principles. He achieved greatness for himself and his entire organization. And most important of all, he followed the universal principle; "WE MUST BUILD TRUE SUC-CESS IN OUR LIVES AND WORK." Do you get the picture?

Here's what I would hope they write about me: "Allan was a kind and gentle man, who always stopped to help those who needed help. He always put others first before himself. He was a loving and compassionate human being. He cared deeply for his children, his grandchildren, and the loves of his life. He valued his friend-ships as he did his family. He always tried to remember the good things about his mother and father. He honored and respected all whom he came in contact with. He was a man of the utmost in-tegrity and trust. He valued, loved and appreciated the woman in his life, Roxanne. He was grateful to all who mentored, supported, healed, and blessed his life while on this earth."

These words are words of hope, because the truth is I am on the path of still fulfilling these noble aspirations, and once the jour-ney ends, I will know that I have achieved what truly is important, not success, but enlightenment.

Buddha says:
"Do not err in this matter of self and other.
Everything is Buddha without exception. Here is
that immaculate final stage, where thought
is pure in its true nature."

Beware of Gurus Bearing Gifts

In my relentless pursuit of learning who I am and what this jour-ney of discovery is all about, people are appearing in my life who are in what I have been calling "purposeful alignment." Recently I met with an old friend, who has now built himself a very success-ful coaching and seminar business. We shared "war stories" about what it's been like to be in business without the self-styled Western gurus lurking in the wings, it was now totally up to us as the captains of our own ships.

We had similar experiences with individuals who ride the roller coaster of fame and fortune and are quite eager to take those of us who are willing along for the ride. We have all met them, and in our desperate need to accomplish something great in our lives – whether it's financial freedom or being recognized as a leader we are willing to give up body and soul to follow them, despite the fact we know that these individuals are ego-based narcissists.

They are known to the Western world, mistakenly, as gurus. Western style gurus come in many forms: self help, motivational, spiritual, medical, sales, marketing, and almost every category of human and business life. Sometimes we humans need a little help getting from point A to point B. Perhaps it's the feeling that we still need the guiding hand of a parent. The truth is that we are by nature followers when it comes to anyone who even remotely appears to replace our parents. It's like we all need a "Moses" to take us to the promised land of milk and honey.

And so the gurus continually show up on our radar screen, until we learn we can actually manage life without them and really be at peace with our own sense of integrity and truth. Only then are we able to design our own destiny. We don't need to live someone else's dream, vision, or reality. As my friend and I began to share stories of life under the shadow of our personal Western style gurus we realized the common theme is one of being dispensable when the Great Guru no longer needs you or you no longer worship the Great Guru. The moment of truth comes when you realize that person is neither a guru, your father, your mother, or the person you think can take you to the top of the mountain. The minute your loyalty and allegiance is in question you're likely to be abandoned. You have to reach the pinnacle yourself.

Another point comes to light here. I have been in search of personal gurus my entire life, and, interestingly enough, they have found me. Every time they have found me I have been in a state of need, and seeking answers and meaning to my life. However, rather than look within, I have always chosen the easier route of having someone else look after me, someone else whom I perceived to have all the answers. And I was willing to pay big bucks to follow this gallivanting guru to the Promised Land, and to have him take me out of the darkness and into the light. Yes, it's difficult to be alone in the dark, whether you are a child or an adult.

The lesson both my friend and I learned was that we can essentially retain all our ideas, maintain our self -respect and integrity, and venture forth alone to accomplish what we were meant to accomplish and what we love to do. We can empower others to do it alone as well. We are merely guides and mentors. And for that reason we need to abolish the term guru in our western society and replace it with the term mentor or guide. I believe strongly in using the term guru only with reference to the Eastern religion definition of the "true" guru. According to Webster's dictionary, the second level of its meaning is that the guru is a spiritual leader, a saint, an Enlightener. Literally the word guru means teacher: GU (darkness) RU (light); One who brings light into darkness. A teacher. However, the meaning of the word Guru in Sikh terminology is at a further higher level, and it stands for the 'prophet.' The practice is based on a long line of Hindu philosophical understandings of the importance of knowledge and that the teacher, guru, is the sacred conduit to self-realization. Till today in India and among people of Hindu or Sikh persuasion, the title retains its significant hallowed space.

The Dalai Lama, speaking of the importance of the guru, said:

> *"Rely on the teachings to evaluate a guru: Do not have blind faith, but also no blind criticism. The guru in Buddhism represents a set of teachings and beliefs stating that no common*

man is a god or a guru and that we are all interconnected to one another to do good and be good. We are to understand that it is through the collaborative efforts of humankind that we will always come from a place of abundance and happiness."

I hope this book serves as a wellspring for your own journey of self-discovery. And I encourage you to write me with your own personal story; it will be printed, with your permission, in a follow-up book. Pay attention to those serendipitous meetings with people who just appear in your life. They are a reminder of the past, a test to see if you'll drink the Kool-Aid again, or have learned your lesson, that you don't need a guru, you simply need a fellow traveler for the journey.

Buddha says:
"Grasping after systems, imprisoned by dogmas for the most part in this world. But he who does not go in for system-grasping he neither doubts nor is perplexed; by not depending on others, knowledge herein comes to be his own."

The Misguided Life of a Recovering MLM Addict

The pressure to succeed can be so strong that you are willing to sacrifice your integrity and your friends to join a multi-level marketing company, and only because somebody told you they were "looking for a few good leaders" to help others become financially independent and successful. And when you go on stage, you pad your monthly earnings, so that others will say; "Well, if he can make it and he's just a truck driver, I can make millions." Then you see your "up line" driving a Jaguar and you're still driving the Volkswagen van, and you wonder what's wrong with this picture.

Next you read a book by Robert Fitzpatrick called *False Profits: Spiritual Deliverance from Multi-level Marketing*, and you find out that only 4 percent of Multi-level Marketing participants actually make any significant money. In their haste to enroll their down line, those above you will never tell you that truth. I've been there; I've been an up line and I am also a recovering MLM addict, having been involved in multi-level companies starting with every letter of the alphabet from Amway to Jewelway. And remember the scorn when you left the tribe – you were banished to the Island of MLM Quitters, the equivalent of a leper colony, and nobody would talk to you or be seen with you. Robert L. Fitzpatrick has spent years investigating the Multi-level Marketing industry; you'll find his take on the pyramid scheme epidemic in chapter 6.

2

Finding the Ultimate Purpose in Your Work and Your Life

It is truly amazing what happens when you begin to live your life on purpose, whatever that purpose is. I began this journey of seeking what my true purpose was about thirty-five years ago. At that time, I was the executive director of Big Brothers. I truly believed that my purpose was to spend the rest of my life in service to fatherless boys. Ten years later I found myself receiving a plaque of appreciation for my ten years of devoted service. At a teary farewell dinner, I said goodbye to the big brothers, little brothers, and staff in attendance. The next month I bought Canada's first Decorating Den franchise with my then wife. The truth is it's not about how you start, it's where you finish.

But the real beginning for me was while I was still a mere fetus in my mother's womb, seemingly a very safe place. As it turns out, however it wasn't. From the start, I was presented with an ongoing series of physical and emotional challenges to overcome.

My mother had German measles during her pregnancy, and I was born with congenital cataracts. I had clear vision for my first seven years, after that I was literally looking through a fog. I had experimental surgery at the age of thirteen, which resulted in the loss of vision of one eye. Thus began a pilgrimage of false hope and broken dreams, as my parents took me to the world's best; the Mayo Clinic, the Eye Centre in Boston, and other facilities in the hopes of restoring my vision. Nothing worked, and eventually I resigned myself to a life of partial blindness.

When I first learned that my optic nerve was damaged and I would go blind, I can recall sitting in my room and feeling this enormous, enveloping presence behind me. I can recall the words, "It's going to be okay, we will look after you." My sense was that in that moment, divine intervention took over, and from that point on my life would never be the same. Whenever I crossed the street, whenever I ran for a bus, whenever there was imminent risk, I would always be protected. When the sight in my other eye began to fail at the age of thirty-seven I was scheduled for surgery, and in order to prepare, I went to psychic healers and did a lot of meditation.

One of the psychic healers who ultimately had a profound impact on my life described the surgery and its positive outcome exactly as it would happen. Indeed, as a result of the surgery I was blessed with 20/20 vision in one eye with a contact lens. I read my doctor's name on his lab coat for the first time. I saw colors, I saw faces, and I saw a blue sky and green grass and lavender flowers.

Clearly it didn't take a book or a lifetime of learning for me to understand how much we need to appreciate what we have rather than what we don't have. For a time, I felt truly blessed. Gradually, however, our world filled with consumption, greed, and ego got in my way again, persuading me that what I had wasn't good enough. So I fell victim to wanting more, achieving more, getting more, buying more, craving more, expecting more. I was caught up in the relentless pursuit of success, as defined by others and inherited by me.

Amongst these pages you will learn of the many coincidental and serendipitous events that have dotted my landscape since I was about thirteen years old. The number of moments of divine intervention are too numerous to mention; suffice to say they took me full circle to where I am today. After years of psychic healing, re-birthing, past life regression, Rolfing, EST, Context Training, psychotherapy, and native chanting, I have finally arrived at the beginning of what my new life will look like. But there is a difference this time. I'm not just trying to fix up my old life. The fact that I recently celebrated my sixty-fourth birthday is in itself a miracle. As Churchill once said: "This is not the end; it is not even the beginning of the end. But it is, perhaps, the end of the beginning." This is the beginning of my life as a Zentrepreneur.

Following Your Passion

Ray Kurzwell, the inventor and futurist once wrote:

"We've seen a migration away from jobs that involve extending our bodies. At the beginning of the twentieth century, thirty percent of the population worked on farms and thirty percent worked in factories. Those figures are now down to three percent each. So we've seen a profound shift there already. Increasingly, professions involve expanding the reach of our minds and creating knowledge. Knowledge in very broad forms, whether the knowledge is music or art or culture or writing or science or technology. Increasingly that's where our work efforts will be directed.

I think people should go with their passion. If they really have a passion for art, we've seen a great empowering of the arts through technology. There's a tremendous need for creating graphics and so on. I know artists that could hardly make a living who are now in tremendous demand as Web designers. It does pay to learn skills to be able to express one's passion in the vernacular and technology of the times. I do have exposure to a variety of fields, and it's remarkable to me how technically sophisticated every field is becoming, from library science to music to art to, certainly, science and technology."

Several years ago I attended a seminar with the renowned speaker and mentor, Jim Rohn. He asked us all what we did for a living, and the responses ranged from chartered accountant to broadcaster. I was the broadcaster. He then asked us what we liked to do most when we were ten years old. Everyone's faces lit up as we went around the room recounting our stories. I recalled that when I was ten, my father built a makeshift radio station in our den, with an amplifier and record player to spin records like a real DJ. It was there in my make believe radio station, broadcasting to my mother on a nine inch speaker in the kitchen that I found true happiness. With my mom as my number one fan I did indeed find my true passion – broadcasting.

Rohn's theory was just this: whatever we loved to do when we were ten years old, was what we would wind up doing at some point in our life. This would become our true passion and our greatest enjoyment. Until that time, we were just doing our jobs. What did you love to do when you were ten years old?

An Oregon company is helping you to find that "passionate" little ten year old again. It is enabling people to stop dreaming and actually live their vision for a couple of days. VocationVacations sets up dream-career holidays for its clients – or, as it calls them their on-the-job adventures. Their website invites us to TEST-DRIVE YOUR DREAM JOB™. They say:

> *"Let's face it, most of us spend the majority of our waking moments at work – and yet few of us are actually doing work that we're passionate about. But who says it has to be that way?"*

They believe "work" can be much, much more than just a four-letter word. That's why they've made it their business to offer a chance to test-drive your dream job with no need to quit your day job. No need to tell the boss. Just spend a couple days on a VocationVacation, working one-on-one with a VocationVacations Mentor, to see what your dream job is really like.

You can take a VocationVacation to truly explore a career change, to sample the "road not taken" or to enjoy a fun, unique learning experience!

Whether your inner voice is telling you to go find your true calling or you're simply curious about a career change, Vocation-Vacations® offers one-of-a-kind holiday adventures that are empowering people everywhere to realize their dreams not only in work, but in life.

While on your VocationVacations® holiday, you'll work alongside an expert mentor who shares your passion and will offer invaluable insights into your dream career. You'll also receive two free sessions with a VocationVacations-affiliated Life/Career Coach."

Imagine how great it would be if every day felt like a Friday.

There is even a testimonial from 70 year old Jim Franklin, Brew Master Vocationer from Port Townsend, Washington, who writes, "I have a passion for taking a different look at my life, because of my VocationVacations experience, I thank your organization for giving me this opportunity for a lasting birthday memory."

Interesting enough, the founder and president of the company, Brian Kurth , was interviewed recently for an article in the *Vancouver Province*, by Elisa Hendricks: "Most people who take a VocationVacation," says Kurth, "are trying on a career they seriously want to pursue." Each VocationVacation is a hands-on experience that lets vocationers sample the reality of their dream job – this isn't job shadowing or a fantasy camp. "After the dot-com bust handed me a pink slip," says Kurth, "I traveled around the country for six months, and everywhere I went, I heard people practically apologizing for what they did for a living...then light up when they talked about their dream career."

"Passions span everything from culinary to animals, sports, fashion, entertainment and even unique career aspirations such as private investigator," says Kurth. The growing success of his venture has spun off into a TV series, *This Job's a Trip*, on the Travel Channel. "There have been a few surprises, like how popular the Dog Daycare VocationVacation is," says Kurth, "but what isn't surprising is that so many people feel unhappily employed and long for work they feel passionate about."

Buddha says:
"Deeds done in harmony with one's path of
life are those which bring clarity and peace
and harmony to the doer."

Right Livelihood

As we build our businesses in an ethical and purposeful way, we are engaging in "purposeful alignment" with everyone we encounter. Given that like attracts like, we will soon begin to attract other purposeful individuals on the same journey.

When we look at the Eightfold Path of Buddha's teachings, we find **Right Livelihood**:

"Right livelihood encourages us to seek a way of sustaining ourselves which minimizes the impact we have on others and the world in general. In gaining our living we may feel that circumstances force us into ignoring such considerations, but Right Livelihood encourages us to think differently, to appreciate the interconnectedness of all things and to tread lightly with due care and compassion."

What's Happened to the Baby Boomers?

If you are a baby boom survivor, you've been raised according to the precepts of Dr. Spock. Not that we can blame Dr. Spock for everything that's gone wrong with the "me" generation. He's only partially responsible. Society has pretty much adapted to this band of boomer renegades, as opposed to the reverse, which is "Enough is Enough."

It's a double-edged sword when you are a baby boomer. You grow up impossibly demanding and hating how demanding all of your fellow boomers are. You become ruthlessly competitive – and even more competitive about appearing noncompetitive.

In a recent article in *Fast Company* magazine, Harriet Rubin, said it best:

> *"Baby boomers were raised on ambition and are a generation that is never happy with what it has. When everything comes too easily, all you want is more. Ambition is the longest unrequited love affair of boomers' lives. It scrambles their brains, and leaves them feeling empty and unfulfilled. No wonder boomers are reaching their forties and fifties and feeling as fried as the Colonel's best."*

In her article she talks about a man named Larry Brilliant. He became CEO of Softnet Systems Inc., a broadband company based in San Francisco that provides high-speed Internet access to communities, and airports. On the surface, Brilliant appears to be a very successful businessman, running a company with four hundred employees that has a market value of $280 million.

But Brilliant asked himself a very critical question that would measure his own ambition. He was quoted as saying, "Where better could I test my soul than in the land of temptation, power, and money?" Silicon Valley.

Writes Rubin: "Brilliant has found a new way to be ambitious, a healthy way, and a way to act ambitiously without letting it sink into his sense of identity. Ambition, after all, is a basically healthy state," when taken literally and used correctly.

"There are people in Silicon Valley who are more successful than Larry Brilliant. And there are people in Silicon Valley who are richer than he is. But there are few who have had more impact on the world at large than he has." Brilliant has devoted the better part of his life to helping save lives in India.

If we look at a Zentrepreneur like Larry Brilliant, Rubin points out that, "Brilliant has been ambitious for one thing only: his soul. How many of us would consider the soul a sufficient driver for success? The soul, after all, can be an annoyance when you're trying to get ahead. But things are changing." As Rubins says: "The soul may be the next drilling platform to plumb the heart of the leader. As the new economy continues, each of us is going to be drilled down to our depths. And the only mark of difference between us will be in our deep identity, our soul. Everything else will be commodified."

That is why Brilliant has devoted his life to understanding that one simple, puzzling mantra: "Live your life without ambition. But live as those who are ambitious." Do that and you discover the discipline of living an authentic life, and of living hard, as if each day counts. "If you live a rich life of the spirit, you are not distracted," says Brilliant. "You carry out your duty, your dharma, no matter what."

Larry Brilliant is not only surviving the dysfunctionality of boomerism, but by contradicting the spiritual deficit of free-market capitalism, he is contributing to a new way of doing business with other like minded Zentrepreneurs in a mythical but somewhat surreal place we might call *Zentropolis*. Ron Rubin and Stuart Avery Gold, in their writings on the subject, say that "an Entrepreneur creates a business, but a Zentrepreneur creates a business and a life."

Buddha says:
"By day the sun shines, and by night shines
the moon. The warrior shines in his armor and
the Brahmin in his meditation. But the Buddha
shines by day and by night–in the brightness
of his glory shines the man who is awake."

So what will it take to wake people up? Not much – they just need a little encouragement and a certain degree of hope and trust that there is an alternative, a different way to look at things that brings happiness and fulfillment, rather than struggle, competition, envy, anger, frustration and the relentless pursuit of more "bling." Stuart Wilde in his many books always says; "Life was not meant to be a struggle." So if it was not meant to be a struggle, what kind of mixed messages did we get from our generation, our parent's generation and their parents before them? Well, all you need to do is pull out an old photo album of your grandparents, provided you are in your sixties like I am. I defy you to find a happy face; I mean, nobody is smiling, not even the kids. And if you really want to see an unhappy bunch take a look at the pictures of the old pioneers. I mean, there's a group of hearty souls who define the word "struggle." Their entire life was built around struggle and survival.

Somewhere between those early days of struggle and our parents reminding us every day that there is no reward unless you put in a hard day's work, we got lost. We got spoiled; I mean that we really got spoiled. Today's definition of a hard day's night would make even the Beatles write a new song. North American society has come up with every conceivable way of making life as easy as possible for us with every conceivable technological apparatus. Whether it's your office, your home, or your car, manufacturers are escalating the pace of production to meet the demands of an "instant gratification" society. Speed is the buzz word: "I'll buy it if I only need to push a button, speak into a receiver, clap my hands, or flash a chip. If I can have everything in the palm of my hands so I don't need to think and just make life easier all around." Then there is the workplace, where benefits rule and the measure of success on the job is not about loyalty or investment of time and energy, it's more about entitlement, socialization, and always looking for an exit strategy. So what's gone wrong? Fundamentally somewhere along the line the message got muted. Today's entrepreneur, as an example, is no farther ahead of Colonel Saunders when he opened his first fast food chicken outlet. The same principles of success apply, yet it seems he was happier, look – he's always smiling.

But seriously, I think what happened was that someone decided that they would associate wealth with success with happiness, and thus "success gurus" were born. In the early days it was Norman Vincent Peale or Dale Carnegie. Then it was Zig Ziegler. Today it's Tony Robbins or Lance Armstrong. On his speaker's site, it says that Lance Armstrong will share his formula for success with you for a cool $40,000 US. His topic "From the Tour de France to the Boardroom – Pushing Your Team to Victory." That's his pitch, "pushing your team to victory" – an interesting paraphrase. Why the need to push to victory or push anything? What's at the end of the rainbow, a pot of gold, or just another end of another rainbow? How many rainbows have you chased, only to find that at the end there is only a temporary sudden rush or feeling of success, but after it's over it's on to the next, and the next, and the next. Victory, success, defeat, winning, achievement, is the language most understood by athletes, like Lance Armstrong, and in the business world.

The analogy to sports has always preoccupied the American psyche, and defining true success has always been measured by the success of America's sporting teams. Those who win World

and gratitude. You could say the real meaning of success is the ability to fulfill your desires effortlessly and with ease.

Yet by itself, success, including the creation of wealth, has been considered by some to be a process that requires hard work, and often at the expense of others. What's needed is a more spiritual approach to success and to affluence, which is the abundant flow of all good things to you.

The Seven Spiritual Laws, developed by Deepak Chopra, have helped many people live in harmony with nature and create with joy, abandon, and love once they have recognized success's true meaning. A law, in the words of Deepak Chopra, "is the process by which the unmanifest becomes the manifest and the process by which the dreamer manifests his dreams." Success could be defined as the "continual expansion of happiness and the progressive realization of worthy goals." It can also be seen as the "ability to fulfill desires with effortless ease. The ultimate true success would be the miraculous."

We have now seen that there are many aspects to success; material wealth is only one component. Moreover, success is a journey, not a destination. Material abundance, just happens to be one of those things that make the journey more enjoyable. But true success in life also includes good health, energy, and enthusiasm for life, fulfilling relationships, creative freedom, emotional and psychological stability, a sense of well being, and peace of mind.

The Journey

As this book has unfolded, I have learned some great lessons, the seven spiritual laws among them, the most important of which is to be patient with your journey. We are each learning to be on a better path in our lives and our work. To do this in our twenties, thirties, forties, or even fifties is an uphill climb given our childhood training and early adulthood programming, but to start at my advanced age is even more of a challenge.

Some of you may question the motivation for this book. In fact, in 2004 I began planning for it, with the working title of *Buddha in the Boardroom*. However, I soon discovered I was not in the right space to begin the journey; I was caught up in the same daily spin that many of us are engaged in until we realize that something is missing. We are chasing that ever elusive state of nirvana that never seems to come.

Money comes and goes; happiness is merely an interruption of sadness; anxiety is caused by fear; business is done to make money; we create relationships to make us happy, but they don't; we are never alone but just "in between" relationships – it's too painful to be alone. We meet and network with people to get business, and we make money to buy things to be happy. But when we're done buying the house, the car, and the big screen TV, the tropical vacation, the winter condo, the summer cottage, and the ski trip we look around and wonder what is next. We're never satisfied.

In 2005, I'd had enough. That didn't mean I planned to drop out and retreat to a monastery in the Himalayas, although I was tempted. I decided to do something different with my life. After connecting with a few people at a deeper level and hearing their stories, observing how effortlessly they conducted their business and personal lives and seeing how truly happy and content they were, I began to investigate how I could begin a similar journey.

This book and the writings herein are only the beginning of that journey. I am not a Buddhist nor am I a deeply religious man; I am, however, deeply spiritual. I've had many life altering experiences that have come through divine intervention and a source that goes beyond the infrastructure of a religious institution. I don't meditate regularly, do yoga or burn candles. I'm very likely much like you, just beginning the journey. And if by some chance I can inspire you to begin the journey with me as a fellow traveler, perhaps we can learn something from each other.

I became intrigued by the Eightfold Path of the teachings of the Buddha and concluded that if we were simply to conduct our lives with these fundamental principles, not only would we be in right alignment, but our life's work would be that of personal choice and fulfillment, businesses would grow and prosper for the right reasons, our relationships would be of pure intention, and our world view would change to embrace each human encounter with equanimity, joy, and love.

Buddha says:
"The moment we are enlightened within, we go
beyond the voidness of a world confronting us."

The Eightfold Path

The Noble Eightfold Path describes the way to the end of suffering, as it was laid out by Siddhartha Gautama. It is a practical guideline to ethical and mental development with the goal of freeing the individual from attachments and delusions, and it leads to understanding the truth about all things. Together with the **Four Noble Truths**:

1. **Life means suffering.** To live means to suffer, because the human nature is not perfect and neither is the world we live in. During our lifetime, we inevitably have to endure physical suffering such as pain, sickness, injury, tiredness, old age, and eventually death; and we have to endure psychological suffering like sadness, fear, frustration, disappointment, and depression.

2. **The origin of suffering is attachment to transient things and the ignorance thereof.** Transient things do not only include the physical objects that surround us, but also ideas, and – in a greater sense – all objects of our perception. Ignorance is the lack of understanding of how our mind is attached to impermanent things. The reasons for suffering are desire, passion, ardor, pursuit of wealth and prestige, striving for fame and popularity, or in short: craving and clinging. Because the objects of our attachment are transient, their loss is inevitable, thus suffering will necessarily follow.

3. **The cessation of suffering is attainable.** The third noble truth expresses the idea that suffering can be ended by attaining dispassion. This means that suffering can be overcome through human activity, simply by removing the cause of suffering. Attaining and perfecting dispassion is a process of many levels that ultimately results in the state of Nirvana. Nirvana means freedom from all worries, troubles, complexes, fabrications and ideas. Nirvana is not comprehensible for those who have not attained it.

4. **There is a path to the end of suffering.** A gradual path of self-improvement. The path to the end of suffering can extend over many lifetimes, and its effects will disappear gradually, as progress is made on the path.

They constitute the essence of Buddhism. Great emphasis is put on the practical aspect, because it is only through practice that one can attain a higher level of existence and finally reach Nirvana. The eight aspects of the path are not to be understood as a sequence of single steps, instead they are highly interdependent principles that should be seen and practiced in relationship with each other.

and peacefully. The Buddha mentions four specific activities that harm other beings and that one should avoid for this reason: 1) dealing in weapons; 2) dealing in living beings (including raising animals for slaughter as well as slave trade and prostitution; 3) working in meat production and butchery, and 4) selling intoxicants and poisons, such as alcohol and drugs. Furthermore, any other occupation that would violate the principles of right speech and right action should be avoided.

6. Right Effort

Right effort can be seen as a prerequisite for the other principles of the path. Without effort, which is in itself an act of will, nothing can be achieved, whereas misguided effort distracts the mind from its task, and confusion will be the consequence. Mental energy is the force behind right effort; it can occur in either wholesome or unwholesome states. The same type of energy that fuels desire, envy, aggression, and violence can fuel self-discipline, honesty, benevolence, and kindness. Right effort is detailed in four types of endeavors that rank in ascending order of perfection: 1) to prevent the arising of unwholesome states; 2) to abandon unwholesome states that have already arisen; 3) to arouse wholesome states that have not yet arisen; and 4) to maintain and perfect wholesome states already arisen.

7. Right Mindfulness

Right mindfulness is the controlled and perfected faculty of cognition. It is the mental ability to see things as they are, with clear consciousness. Usually, the cognitive process begins with an impression induced by perception or by a thought, but then it does not stay with the mere impression. Instead, we almost always conceptualize sense impressions and thoughts immediately.

Right mindfulness is anchored in clear perception, and it penetrates impressions without getting carried away. Right mindfulness enables us to be aware of the process of conceptualization in a way that we actively observe and control the direction of our thoughts. Buddha accounted for this as the four foundations of mindfulness: 1) contemplation of the body; 2) contemplation of feeling (repulsive, attractive, or neutral; 3) contemplation of the state of mind; and 4) contemplation of the origination, the components, the development and decline of things, when we can find a deep understanding in the nature of ourselves, and to know our own hearts is to know the hearts of others.

8. Right Concentration

The eighth principle of the path, right concentration, refers to the development of a mental force that occurs in natural consciousness, although at a relatively low level of intensity, namely concentration. Concentration in this context is described as single pointedness of mind, meaning a state where all mental faculties are unified and directed onto one particular object. Right concentration for the purpose of the Eightfold Path means wholesome concentration, that is, concentration on wholesome thoughts and actions. The Buddhist method of choice to develop right concentration is through the practice of meditation. The meditating mind focuses on a selected object. It first directs itself onto it, then sustains concentration, and finally intensifies concentration step by step. Through this practice it gradually becomes natural to apply elevated levels of concentration to everyday situations.

The Karma of Purposeful Alignment

As we move along the path toward enlightenment, we will meet
people who will have a profound impact on the outcome of our
lives. Nothing is by accident in the order of things. There is an old
expression: If you want to make God laugh, tell him you have a
plan. So when people cross your path, never question the reason,
just let go and see what happens. Whatever your karma is in this
lifetime, all manner of individuals will be brought to you to test
you on how well you handle things this time around. How you
conduct your life, your business, and your relationships will determine your happiness in the present moment. Also, whatever your
mission and purpose in life becomes, those individuals who are on
the same path will be brought to you in support of that mission.
You can call it synchronicity, an accident, serendipity, coincidence,
fate; I call it *purposeful alignment.*

3

Awakening the Buddha Within

Kate Taylor in a recent article in the *Seattle Times* wrote:

"An unprecedented number of Americans have turned to Buddhism – there are now an estimated six million Buddhists nationwide – more and more Buddhist ideas and symbols are popping up in bookstores, gift shops, and business retreats it's also thriving in boardrooms, shopping malls, and cyberspace.

A shopper, for example, can find Buddha T-shirts, Buddha key chains, Buddha photo holders, books that coach readers to become a bodhisattva (person on the path to enlightenment), music for Buddhist meditation, and a Buddha ball that shoots beams of light. And that's just from one mall, Washington Square Mall in Tigard, Oregon."

In her article she quoted observations from a number of American Buddhist leaders.

Robert Beatty, leader of the Portland Insight Meditation Community said: "Every time Buddhism enters a culture, it transforms the culture. What's happening now is there's this deep flowing into our culture of rather significant Buddhist practices, and along with that come the accoutrements."

"Some of those accoutrements are sleazy and cheap," said Charles Prebish, Pennsylvania State University professor of religion studies and author of scores of books and articles about Buddhism.

Our Journey

Along the spiritual journey in Buddhism, there are two aspects of the path that reflect two distinct kinds of practice one must engage in. Though the Buddha taught both, they were passed along over the centuries from teacher to students in two separate lineages.

What does it mean to open the heart? First of all, we understand that the idea of the heart is a metaphorical one. The heart is perceived in most cultures to be the wellspring of compassion, love, sympathy, righteousness, and intuition, and intuition rather than merely the muscle responsible for circulating blood through the body. In the Buddhist worldview, both aspects of the heart, however, are understood to take place in the mind. Ironically, the Buddhist view is that the mind is located in the middle of the chest. An open heart is an open mind. A change of heart is a change of mind. Still, our conception of the heart provides a useful, if temporary, tool when trying to understand the distinction between the "vast" and "profound" aspects of the path."

America's Heart and Mind

In response to the tragedy and disaster in Hurricane Katrina, Americans "opened their hearts" to embrace the victims with offers of food, water, shelter, jobs, and education. North Americans by nature are a generous lot, especially when it comes to a national calamity.

If we look at the Buddhist view of an open heart being an "open mind," the question is, will the perceived notion of generosity change the minds of those who are helping?

The poverty level amongst Afro Americans is self evident, as is the government view of poor African-Americans with no money, no jobs, and no education. They are thus prime candidates for recruitment to fight America's wars abroad. This is an interesting turning point; it may change the minds and perceptions of much of the American populace. I would encourage you to see the highly acclaimed Oscar winning movie *Crash* which paints a truer picture of America's mindset.

As we journey toward a new sense of zenlightenment, we must begin to "open our minds" by opening our hearts. Recently, I have had many occasions to test my response to people and events. In one case I failed miserably, by allowing anger to ruin my evening. I succeeded in another case, by opening my heart to my partner in life and by changing my mind about how I would share my deepest fears with her.

Whether it's your wife, your husband, your boss, your business partner, your clients, or your friends, the opportunity you have now is to test your open mindedness. Can you view these people in a different way, a new way that enriches your experience with them? Making that fundamental shift requires a new way of thinking. Be patient with yourself and gradually you'll be able to make these subtle changes in your life.

> *Buddha says:*
> *"Train yourself in this way: from higher to higher,*
> *from strength to strength we will strive, and we*
> *will come to realize unsurpassed freedom."*

Kooky Koot

During my work with the Big Brothers organization I met Jon-Lee Kootnekoff, the former head coach of the Simon Fraser University basketball team. Jon was an intense, competitive individual who believed that life was all about winning. One night he collapsed at courtside during a game, was taken to the hospital, and, while recuperating, he experienced a revelation that would change his life forever. Now this was not a "religious" experience, nor was it a self-induced shot of awareness. It was best described as an awakening.

He finally truly understood what he was supposed to be doing, and it wasn't coaching basketball. Jon has spent his entire life since then empowering individuals to take control of their own personal journey, through words, study, meditation, and a belief in a higher source. If we allow it, that higher source directs us, if only we stand aside.

Don't wait until you have a massive heart attack, get cancer, or wind up in a wheelchair to experience the awakening as to what your real *purpose* is.

Jon, was known in those early days as "Kooky Koot." Little did he know that thirty-five years later his theories would become mainstream in a movement known as "New Age."

As my first mentor, Jon inspired me to look at life differently from what I'd been taught by my parents, my teachers, my religion, and indeed the world. The world was simply not ready for Kooky Koot thirty-five years ago. Today, more and more people are choosing to look at the world differently just like Kooty does.

Choose Wisely

This past year I have had many occasions to share my zentrepreneurial thoughts with a good friend of mine, Bruce Stewart. Bruce was equally inspired to share his own thoughts and thus we forged an even stronger friendship. We are never alone on our journey if it is the "right" journey. When you make the "right"

decisions about your livelihood and it is one of contribution and purpose, divine intervention will bring to you all manner of people and resources to help you accomplish whatever it is you are doing for the highest good.

Perhaps you're asking how this applies to business, your clients and your customers. If your sole motivation is to make money, they become just a means to an end. When they realize that you've put money first and them second, they will abandon you. If your company is on a mission to make money first, bilk people second, and lie to shareholders, you will be plagued with setbacks, both moral and financial, and you'll eventually be discovered. You will pay the ultimate price just like Enron and WorldCom. Choose your path carefully and wisely, and in the same way, choose your business partners/associates and friends wisely. Jim Rohn, says, "You become the average of the five people you hang out with the most, so choose them carefully." You will become their average financially, spiritually, ethically, and morally.

Those of us who embark on spiritual paths are motivated in different ways: some of us want to know the unknowable, others want to know themselves, and still others want to know everything. Some people want transformation, while others want miracles; many want to alleviate suffering, help others, and leave the world a better place.

Most of us are seeking love or fulfillment in one way or another. Everyone wants inner peace, acceptance, satisfaction, and happiness. We all want genuine remedies for feelings of despair, alienation, and hopelessness. Don't we all want to find spiritual nourishment and healing, renewal and a greater sense of meaning? Contrary to what some may think you don't awaken the Buddha within by attending a weekend retreat at Deepak's in San Diego, nor by purchasing a set of tapes from an infomercial guru at 2 a.m. As you would have on any successful voyage you'll need at least a road map, a compass, and a knowledge of the truck stops along the way.

Hopefully, as you join me on my own personal journey of discovery and transformation, we will together seek to awaken the Buddha within and achieve the same happiness in business and in life that we so richly deserve.

Buddha says;
"Hidden in the mystery of consciousness,
the mind, incorporeal, flies alone far away.
Those who set their mind on harmony
become free from the bonds of death."

4

Zenlightened Leadership

Leaders learn experientially, not theoretically. So what then, are the experiences zenlightened leaders need to learn to succeed in business and in life? Zenlightened leaders such as Arran Stephens, the very essence of the 21st century Zentrepreneur of the new world of doing business need to tell their stories.

The Arran Stephens Story

Arran Stephens started his entrepreneurial journey on 4th Avenue in Vancouver decades ago (1967) as the owner of a vegetarian, natural foods restaurant. In those early days he was known as the "hippie capitalist." Today he's the CEO and Founder of North America's largest producer of organic cereals, Nature's Path Foods Inc. (www.naturespath.com). He runs his company much like his life. "It's all a journey" – and he adheres to a strict code of ethics. "Treat the soil like you would your own children....with tender loving care and they will grow healthy and nurtured." Arran begins every day before dawn with meditation during which time he says he receives inner guidance and wisdom to take on the challenge of learning from each day and running a 125+ million dollar company (growing at 25% per annum) that spans the globe.

Since the beginning, his wife and family have not only been at his side but have been valued co-workers as well. They share a compelling faith in a higher source and purpose – and their lives reflect that.

Shareholders who might have thought that by hiring a Zen thinking CEO would have been a recipe for disaster, cutting into profits
and efficiency of operation – are now embracing the humbler
"enlightened leader" in an attempt to distance themselves from
the Jeffrey Skillings of Enron, the Bernie Ebbers of WorldCom
and the Conrad Black syndrome. Creating profits with integrity is
replacing profits for greed. Examining a company's charitable giving record and its view on a sustainable environment are just as
important to a prospective employee today as to whether or not
they get their birthday off, a dental plan or a lock up rack for their
bike. The ethical track record of today's company is increasingly
important to the enlightened consumer as well.

Arran describes himself as a wayfarer or a seeker. He does not
consider himself enlightened, although some others may think
otherwise. His mode is more of a servant-leader. He started his
quest for truth in his early teens, when life lost its purpose and
he hit the streets. Suffering and mistakes became his tutors; he
became addicted to substances and almost perished. At 17, he
took refuge in a monastery to recuperate, and wherein he had a
profound unsought mystical experience. That started a search for
answers to life's meaning, and to understand his encounters with
a mysterious – and what he describes as, "a great light" within. In
his search and studies, he began to put into practice higher standards and disciplines that nurtured the inner life. He overcame
his addictions and never turned back.

Mentors began to have a profound impact in his life and business.
"So long as I live, so long do I learn," was a message from one of
them. Service before self is a very important component of any
spiritual path, and he took that to heart. His search led him to
understand and embrace sustainable living and business models,
organic food production methods, and an abiding respect and
support for the natural environment. While growing up, his parents served as fine examples of this practice. His mother loved to
serve the sick and elderly and his father was a nature lover, early

organic farmer as well as an aspiring writer of songs extolling the earth and cycles of nature. They were very artistic and spiritual in their own way, but not particularly religious.

At the age of 60, when Arran was 13, his father Rupert sold the farm and the family moved to Hollywood where dad pursued his new vocation as a lyricist. Some of his songs were recorded by Ricky Nelson, Lou Rawls, and others. He was never quite monetarily successful in the music field, and it was the general consensus that Rupert was just too good and simple for Hollywood and such a cutthroat business. After some years in Hollywood, his parents moved back to a simpler life on Vancouver Island, where they grew a prolific garden and continued writing songs.

Arran started in business with an art gallery in West Vancouver, called the East West Gallery in 1966, and then in 1967 after spending seven months in India with his beloved spiritual mentor, Sant Kirpal Singh Ji, he returned to Vancouver, fired up with the desire to create an ideal working environment and help people eat better for health. The best way to accomplish this, he believed, was to open up Vancouver's first vegetarian restaurant.

He only had $7 when he got back from India, so he stayed with friends in the Kitsilano neighborhood, a hippie hotbed at the time. One friend loaned him $500 and a relative loaned him $1000. With the $7 in hand along with the $1500 of borrowed money he went out and bought the assets of a bankrupt restaurant and put it all together and started the "Golden Lotus" on West 4th Avenue.

After much hard work the restaurant became successful and served as a model for other altruistic and successful enterprises that followed and which were begun by former employees: the enduring Naam Restaurant and the highly successful Banyen Books. In 1971 Arran started Vancouver's first natural foods supermarket (Lifestream Natural Foods) which evolved into a dynamic profitable enterprise that by 1981, employed over one hundred

company aligned individually and collectively so that all of their practices are best practices in the area of sustainability, waste reduction and efficiency.

Nature's Path recently donated $20,000 to two schools in the poorer districts of Vancouver to establish organic gardens for use by students. This involved tearing up asphalt so that kids could get their hands in the soil growing flowers and vegetables – which Arran feels will help channel their energies away from negative to positive pursuits and a love and appreciation of nature.

> "We'd like to see kids make the connection between their food and the earth, and just how much fun it is to grow delicious plants in living, fertile soil. We want kids to realize that food didn't grow in a supermarket. It's cool to learn composting, saving seeds, and valuing what we all take for granted: our precious food supply."

Arran Stephens sees money as 'green energy' to be used for good or ill:

> "Money is material; it's not inherently evil, for the root of good and evil lies in the mind and heart of us all. We are defined by our choices. If we lack a vision, money and power corrupt us. We need vision and principles that do not change as the world changes around us. Thus, from a more enlightened centre within, we can use money for great good, or, if selfish and greedy, we can use it to harm and congeal."

Arran has quietly and consistently maintained that he didn't get into business to create personal wealth, but instead, it was to earn an honest livelihood; to be an instrument for positive change and to serve the greater good. Along the path and through trial and error, he learned that if an enterprise is not run profitably, it will fail, as so many others have failed. And, a failed business is unable to help anyone. Therefore, at Nature's Path, there is an equal focus on the "financially viable" component of the triple-bottom line.

As the good book says, 'If you're not a profit, you're a loss!' "Obviously, Nature's Path makes a profit, and I am very grateful for the benefits that profitability confers." Further, he emphasizes the importance of giving back in a variety of ways, "a minimum of 10% of time and 10% of earnings. At the end of the day, or by the end of our life, I hope we can say, as dad taught on the farm, 'Always leave the Earth better than you found it.' He quotes a saying from Darshan, one of his mentors, who himself held a position of great trust: 'the purpose of power is to protect.'"

The hippie capitalist has indeed evolved into an enlightened entrepreneur and leader.

Clearly, zenlightened leaders create zenlightened companies that in turn create 21st century *zenployees* who will be the early pioneers for the creation of an idealistic but quite real place, *Zentropolis* – enlightened communities in which to work and live. The closest we can come to "Nirbana" (Nirvavana) – heaven on earth! As Arran Stephens says, "look after your children and they will grow to be nurtured and healthy."

Hidden Companions

For two years Yves Farges, the founder & CEO of Qualifirst Foods and I exchanged e-mails but never met. He was traveling extensively and was unable to accept an invitation to join a Mastermind group I was facilitating of CEOs, and business owners. When he received the press release announcing my book project, he was so pleased to have someone articulate what he had already begun to experience on his own life's journey, that he felt compelled to write to me.

We met for the first time in September of 2005, and this was not your customary interview. We did in fact connect at a deeper level, so I'd like offer you this inner-view of Yves Farges.

It's not unusual for people who grow up in a business family to take it for granted that a business career is also what they will pursue. Farm-Net Importers was founded by Yves Farges' parents in 1957.

He bought it from them in 1999. But his entrepreneurial journey did not begin there. In 1984 Farges began cooking in a basement in Toronto with ten boxes of fine foods and a good suit. The journey began slowly but methodically, much like his cooking style. He would hire sales people by asking them The Question: "Would you rather be the eggs or the bacon? You would rather be the bacon," he told them, "because the chicken only participates, but the pig is committed." He went on his own personal pilgrimage, giving up things like television because he said he had better things to do. "Work becomes a pleasure," he said, "and if you've got a message and a philosophy, then you're really not doing it for the money."

A wise old grandmother with a young soul told him, "If you pursue money, it runs away from you, if you ignore it, it runs toward you." The only way you can become prosperous is to understand money: use it as both a tool and a currency. Today, Farges owns three companies and all the profits are poured back into the companies. He claims it takes greater energy to sell on quality than on price. "There is now an awakening in North America, to food," he says. "People are getting more connected to what they eat. They are recognizing spiritual values inherent in the food they eat. People eat a chocolate bar and they are getting a sugar rush – that's it! Nowadays they are looking at fine food as enhancing their life-feeding parts of them that aren't physical." Cooking for friends and family is a real joy for Farges, and he does it on a higher level. We are filling a spiritual need to make it richer. Eating therefore becomes a "religious" experience.

"Enjoy competition," Farges says, "because when you learn, you win!" That's why he enjoys chess. Just as with chess, as you improve and as time passes the nature of life becomes richer and thus allows you to enjoy it more. In turn, you experience more, and experience is an essential part of life for growth. He attributes the success of his enlightened journey to hidden companions. "Many people," he says, "are doing good for the wrong reason, but as you progress along the path, you realize that intellectual giving can become more elegant and much more satisfying than blowing your own horn."

Farges' first charitable gift, when he was in his early teens, was to the Jerry Lewis telethon, but even then, he asked himself, what did I really do here? It was a good thing to do, but is that all there is? "The act of giving is a complex equation," says Farges. "I think it's very important to broaden the category of giving to include non-monetary giving. When you see a car broken down on the side of the road and you stop and ask them if they need some help, that's giving, and it's good to do a little of that because it elevates you. Farges goes on to explain that in doing such a so-called good deed your life takes on more meaning and purpose.

You realize that while you are on this enlightened path, you have unique opportunities. For people who can truly give, those opportunities appear out of thin air, because hidden companions will also appear out of thin air. I asked him if he felt that somehow we are all connected in this universe to all those hidden companions and whether he believes in purposeful alignment. Yes, he says, we are all connected. "We are all parts of that web and we are all visual creatures. We are all connected through our sincerity and interpersonal relationships."

At a business level, Farges believes that even if the marketplace is crowded there's always room for one more, but if you have only one or two competitors you are in for the fight of your life. Yves Farges, is forty-seven years old. His basic premise of life has been to achieve a state of grace, by being open, enthusiastic, and passionate

ate about what he is doing. Small business, he says, starts off as a solitary path, and becomes much more personal than the corporate world.

Farges and I spent a great deal of our time together discussing how his personal philosophy of life is so interwoven into his business life, that eventually, it all simply and effortlessly becomes one. In his words:

> *"You start being about your team, about your customers, about growing, and about succeeding because your concept is good. The hours are long, but because the business path is a chosen personal path, it does not matter. So am I saying that starting a small business is like a walk in the park? It is hard, incredibly hard, yet thousands of people embark on this journey and start a small business every year. But it is not a walk in the park; it is a pilgrimage.*

> *You embark on a personal pilgrimage to enlighten the business world that your idea works and should succeed. You work to bend decisions in your favor so your small business and the people work within it flourish. You give up many things because small business requires a person's ultimate capital: time.*

> *Watching television and other passive hobbies lost much of their appeal for me when I launched my first small company because it was much more fun tackling the challenges that business throws your way on a daily, sometimes hourly basis. Your friends start to emerge out of the mass of customers you interact with as business becomes truly a seamless part of your life. Work is part of you on this level and satisfaction is a job well done no matter what the task is.*

> *On this path you have company. You have your team – the people you work with. You have the customers that depend on you. You have your suppliers that value your contribution to their own*

pilgrimages. This is quite a crowd on what many believe to be a solitary endeavor, but the reality is that you are leading many.

You also have "hidden companions" on your business journey, and these are the good acts that will benefit from your positive intervention. When, early in my business I gave product away to help out a reception for a women's shelter in Toronto, it was the right thing to do and involved a customer, so the action fit. I did not do it to get more business; I did it because it was a good act. I was surprised when new business appeared out of thin air because of that reception. Product for a silent auction, free product to a young film producer that was tied to a microscopic budget, the list grows long. Your hidden companions will benefit you and your actions and improve the world. So business is a path that is crowded with friends and paved with ethical stones."

Buddha Talks Business

The inspiration to write my book has come from a great variety of people, many of whom I will acknowledge throughout the book. They are authors, writers, broadcasters, and journalists, who themselves are on their own journey of discovery and enlightenment. Through their journalistic endeavors they are inspiring others to tell their own truths of what is important to them. Lynn Brewer, who wrote the best-selling book on the collapse of Enron, and Joel Bakan, creator of the award winning book and film *The Corporation* are just a couple of the many I am grateful to for their courageous efforts to tell the truth.

Buddha says:
"Let him first find what is right and then he can teach it to others, thus avoiding useless pain."

In a January, 2004 article in *Expert Magazine,* entitled "Buddha Talks Business" Jim Schaffer talks about what's gone wrong with business:

> *"Most of us have tried hard to be good corporate citizens. We've dutifully absorbed the lessons we've been taught along the way, both in the course of doing our jobs as well as from the pages of each year's hot business books. The trouble is, not only is much of this wisdom just plain wrong, it may also be preventing you from being successful and could be ruining your health, to boot!"*

This book has been about a new awakening and new thinking to the way we do business. However, as you have been reading you will notice that these cutting edge principles and ideas for business in the 21st century actually stem from 2,500 years ago, in the time of Buddha.

If we slow down rather than speed up as we have all been programmed to do, your mind can operate from a place of peacefulness rather than hectic turmoil. With a quiet mind and a curious, open heart, you'll be able to act more swiftly than your adrenaline-addicted competitors.

Having to be in control all the time isn't just a trait as part of your astrological sign, or a personality dysfunction inherited from one of your parents, it's considered one of the "rules of the game" we talked about earlier. If you're in control, you are in the driver's seat to control your destiny. Or so we think. However to surrender, should not be confused with defeat or failure.

Being in the flow has now been proven to be far more effective in making business decisions. Besides, controlling is time consuming and a waste of energy. Pay attention, observe, and act rather than react in concert with what is already happening. Stay in the present, because that's all there is. The past is gone in a heartbeat, the future is entirely unknown, so all there is is NOW, and there is tremendous personal power in knowing how to use the present moment to the fullest.

Contrary to popular belief your business will not be easier to run by taking a crash course on time management. There is no such thing as time management; it really boils down to how we choose to process our lives. You need to be aware of your own bio-rhythm. Some days are diamonds, some days are gold. It's perfectly natural to wake up on Monday and feel totally rested and feeling at your peak. You approach your business that day with enthusiasm and gusto. Not knowing that on Wednesday morning you feel the direct opposite. It's a simple matter of becoming aware of your own high and low energy cycles, and working with them. Be good to yourself and the world will take care of itself.

Take time out to literally "smell the roses." Make sure you celebrate on anything you have accomplished, no matter how small. Celebrate in the moment; don't wait for a party or gift to arrive. Learn to savor daily tasks and always come from an attitude of gratitude. Be aware that your business will run in cycles, up and down, but you don't have to be like an empty raft in ten foot swells. Stop striving and try to stay on an even keel and you'll plateau rather than rise and fall with every issue or challenge. Besides you are far more effective as a calm, rational leader who is in the flow, rather than an over reactive, compulsive and controlling CEO (Chief Emotional Officer).

The business world is moving at the speed of light to catch up with advanced technology. It should be the reverse, but it's not, and so there is tremendous pressure that is forcing companies to buy into this frenzied belief system; that if they don't stay in the cyber race or even ahead of their competitors they'll lose. In the new world of doing business, high touch will replace high tech as the single most important criteria for change. It's already starting to happen. The GenXers generation is starting to discover that they can't have intimate relationships through e-mail and chat rooms, they are feeling alienated, disenfranchised, missing intimacy. So they are returning to religion, to Buddhism, to anything that will give them a connected feeling.

Clients and customers are no different. They don't want to be put on hold any more and wind up in voice mail hell. They want to talk to a real person on the line, not a digitally mastered voice. They want to talk to a real person when their order at Amazon can't be found. They want to talk to a real person about their phone bill. Everybody wants somebody to talk to; that's why there will always be demand for open line radio shows.

No matter how efficient we become, human contact and relationships will still drive the business world. Make sure you connect with your clients or customers on a personal level and "listen." Avoid corporate jargon and confusing rhetoric to defend your case. The old adage of the customer always being right has given way to arrogance and rudeness. When a customer hangs up, you either have a friend for life or a disgruntled bull loose in a china shop. Which one is going to hurt you the most?

Make your business and your life clear of judgments. Who made you Judge Judy anyway? Stay open and keep learning as long as possible. Don't gossip or hold on to judgments. Your business relationships come down to a fundamental issue of trust and integrity. Therefore you need only ask one question of anyone; what part of this is a lie?

We in this debt ridden North American consumer world have it backwards. We focus on having rather than being. Buddhism talks about karma: "What you ultimately receive is returned to you according to the way you express who you are." As we enter this new era of zenlightened capitalism, there is hope that we will change our habits. Madison Avenue will always try to lure us away from our noble pursuits. Credit card companies will continue to send free credit cards to seniors at high school and rap stars will continue to encourage Afro Americans to "Get Rich or Die Tryin."

So what's going to change the "rules of the game." It starts with one small step, just like a walk on the Moon. It starts with a Toronto, Ontario black man who has begun to try to change the attitudes of young people his age from anger and frustration, and entitlement, to singing a different tune.

Go to Toronto's Yonge Street shopping area on any given day, and you will find groups of tough-looking young men. Their dress is the dress of the urban ghetto culture: puffy down jackets, baseball caps or toques, baggy pants, expensive running shoes. The tunes on their music players glorify violence and demean women. They speak in the same slang you might find on the streets of inner-city Chicago or Detroit. Their role models are "gangsta" rappers like 50 Cent.

BLING is Bring Love in Not Guns, a movement organized by the Black Youth Coalition Against Violence, which brings together many student groups, some of them University of Toronto-based. The Black Students' Association at U of T has been instrumental in organizing the summit. Its president, Kofi Hope, who is also the founder of the Black Youth Coalition Against Violence, hopes the summit will result in meaningful concrete action to help stop the violence. He stressed, though, that the summit is not a response to any particular shooting but a "response to a continual problem that has deep-seated root causes."

How many times have you gone ahead with a decision in your business that you regretted? In hindsight you say I should have trusted my gut. Your gut talking to you is really a *feeling*, and more importantly something called *intuition*. I know researchers say women have it more than we do, but the truth is we all have it. It's just that men try to think digitally not emotionally, so we don't like to use it in the business world. We have been trained at

The MBA program at Stanford University distinguished itself not only by offering a large number of courses that addressed social and environmental issues in business, but also by the relatively large proportion of students who actually took those classes.

The report is the only global survey that evaluates MBA programs for their efforts to prepare graduates on social and environmental stewardship in business.

Buddha says:
"The glorious chariots of kings wear out,
and the body wears out and grows old; but
the virtue of the good never grows old, and thus
they can teach the good to those who are good."

Compassion and Business

What is compassion? Compassion is the wish that others be free of suffering. It is by means of compassion that we aspire to attain enlightenment. It is compassion that inspires us to engage in the virtuous practices that lead to Buddhahood. We must therefore devote ourselves to developing compassion.

The challenge for all of us who are just starting on this path is to take the first step. In the first step toward a compassionate heart, we must develop our empathy or closeness to others. In a society that is increasingly becoming impersonal through technology, this becomes a major challenge. With cell phones, text messaging, e-mail, voice mail, and the Internet, we may never need to be with anyone at a face to face level.

Buddha says, "We must also recognize the gravity of their misery. The closer we are to a person, the more unbearable we find that person's suffering." The closeness he speaks of is not a physical proximity, nor need it be an emotional one. It is a feeling of responsibility, of concern for a person. In order to develop such closeness, we must reflect upon the virtues of cherishing the well-being of others.

We must come to see how this brings inner happiness and peace of mind. We must come to recognize how others respect and like us as a result of such an attitude toward them. We must contemplate the short-comings of self-centeredness, seeing how it causes us to act in unvirtuous ways and how our own present fortune takes advantage of those less fortunate.

It is also important that we reflect upon the kindness of others. This realization is also a fruit of cultivating empathy. We must recognize how our fortune in business is really dependent upon the cooperation and contribution of others. Every aspect of our present well-being is due to hard work on the part of others. As we look around us at the buildings we live and work in, the roads we travel, the clothes we wear, or the food we eat, we must acknowledge that all are provided by others. None of these would exist for us to enjoy and make use of were it not for the kindness of so many people unknown to us. As we contemplate in this manner, our appreciation for others, our empathy and closeness to them increases.

When we look at our business, whether we are owners or workers, the same lessons apply. It is important to recognize the contributions of everyone from the receptionist to the janitor. These are not paid servants, they are persons of value. When we begin to have that equal level of compassion for everyone who touches us, we can begin to look at the success of our business not from a financial standpoint but from a very personal place of deep caring for our fellow travelers on the journey of life.

The next time you have a sales meeting, a senior management strategy session, an employee retreat, or a shareholders' meeting, take the time to really recognize your dependence on your colleagues. This recognition brings about compassion, in turn bringing them even closer. It requires sustained attention to see others through less self-centered lenses. You need to work at recognizing their enormous impact on your well-being both personally and in your business. When you resist indulging in a self-centered view of the world, you can replace it with a worldview that takes every living being into account. We must expect our view of others to change suddenly.

When there are 30 million Americans who make the minimum wage of $5.15 per hour, it's no wonder that the pursuit of money is equated with not just happiness, but survival. These people are referred to as the "working poor." And the gap between the very rich and the very poor is getting wider and wider. Eventually there will be no middle class in America, and homelessness and begging once thought of as a nuisance to be dealt with by local authorities will become epidemic. Unfortunately to everyone's amazement they will become the people you know; the vice presidents and the middle management of corporate America, who after living pay cheque to pay cheque, and credit card to credit card to pursue the American dream, will suffer the humiliation of a lost job, lost income, lost home, and lost possessions. Most Americans will suffer the same humiliation and fate of their next door neighbor. Compassion for others will be the only salvation for a nation that prides itself on being the land of opportunity, not the land of failure.

When Donald Trump fires someone on *The Apprentice*, he says, "It's not personal, it's business!" The truth is, Donald, it is personal, very personal!

Buddha says:
"And those in high thought and in deep contemplation, with ever-living power advance on the path, they in the end find nirvana, the supreme peace and infinite joy."

Zen and Business

Marshall Goldsmith is incorporating Buddha principles in his consulting practice with a high degree of success. The American Management Association named Marshall as one of the fifty great thinkers and leaders who have influenced the field of management over the past eighty years. He ends every e-mail he writes with *"Life is good"* and says: "There are many schools of Buddhist thought. My Buddhist philosophy can be summarized in three simple words, 'Be happy now.' In my mind, this is heaven, this is hell and this is Nirvana. It is not "out there." It is "in here."

> *"The great Western disease is 'I'll be happy when.' This is fueled by our prevailing art form – the commercial. The commercial says, 'You are unhappy, you spend money. You become happy!' I don't believe that anyone can become happy by having more. I also don't believe that anyone can become happy by having less. We can only find happiness and satisfaction with what we have. Life is good when we make it good."*

His coaching philosophy is based upon the same Buddhist principles. He believes that we have no 'fixed identity' but instead we are changing. His coaching approach involves helping people let go of the past and focus on becoming what they want to become.

Buddha says:
"The perfect way knows no difficulties
except it refuses to make preferences."

The New Zenployee

Using the teachings of Buddha in real-world workplace situations will inspire employees, employers, and executives alike with practi-

nology and information-processing industries. When the Internet becomes better understood, it might indeed change American attitudes about the connections between peacetime and prosperity.

Our current fascination with Buddhism goes beyond fad and fashion. We may be gradually recognizing the downside of our violence-prone lifestyle, which not only drains our national budget but infects our households, schools, neighborhoods, theaters, diets, hospitals, and television sets.

At the same time, we seem to be learning to enjoy the upside of our creative business culture, which brings greater pleasure, comfort, health, and knowledge within our reach. Buddhists consider true happiness to be a realistically attainable goal of human life and applaud the creation of wealth as the foundation that makes possible the institutional and individual efforts to attain that goal. The dawn of the 21st century may, in fact, be the ideal moment for business to recognize the long history, and long-term market potential, of awakening.

Is it possible in our present economic environment to create workplaces where social, emotional, spiritual and intellectual needs of individuals are met? As employers or investors, does our responsibility run deeper than economic equation and a purely competitive relationship? One place to look for guidance in response to these questions, is to the ancient wisdom of the Buddha.

Buddhism is not against free enterprise. It does, however, suggest that there be a much closer and deeper relationship between financial gain and the well-being of society. How business profit contributes to the betterment of the community/society is the issue. Shareholders and business leaders have, in Buddhist thinking, a responsibility to create an ethically-based holistic community within their organization and contribute to creating a better society. This is not an issue of philanthropy; it is an issue of intention.

> *"The critical difference between our present business model and*
> *Buddhism relates to the idea of intention" says Dr. Lloyd Field,*
> *CEO of Performance House Ltd. "If our intentions are motivated*
> *by greed, hatred, or delusion, the outcome of those intentions*
> *and the actions prompted by them will inevitably be human suf-*
> *fering, and this includes our own personal condition. Suffering*
> *is the lack of 'will' to do good, it is also distress, pain, poverty,*
> *illness, and so on. Free Enterprise has a limited code of values/*
> *ethics as part of its ethos – what values there are come from a*
> *society's legal systems."*

I believe we are entering an era of Zenlightened Capitalism, where the bottom line is no longer the only reason to be in business. The Noble Eightfold Path of Buddhism is an appropriate starting point to bring Buddhism into the Boardroom, thereby drawing a connection between our economic system and dharma.

Right Action

When we look at the Eightfold Path in the teachings of Buddha, we can identify ways in which we conduct our life and our business and quickly determine if we are in right action. Morality involves speech, action and the way we gain our livelihood. Right Speech concerns the truth, holding the words of truth in mind, and speaking from the truth in a way that is honest. This doesn't mean that these words remain as a set of ideas which we as individuals have identified with and tried to claim. These are the words of truth discovered in experience and spoken in a way that causes no harm.

Words are all important. Our experience of the world is forged out of the ideas we carry with us. If we avoid not only lying to others but also lying to ourselves, everything will not only be freed from the distortions we have imposed but will become purified and therefore more translucent and luminous.

Right Action is a direct result of refined ideas. If our words are of the nature of greed, hatred, and delusion then must our actions be likewise. How different are actions that arise out of their opposites: generosity, compassion, and understanding.

Right Action in business is no different than Right Action in life- they are all intertwined. In our personal lives, in order to accomplish those goals we see essential to our success, we sometimes "push the envelope," so to speak. It's called skillful manipulation. How many of you have done this? By telling people what they want to hear as opposed to what you really believe is the truth. Politics and sales sometimes are kindred partners in crime.

The dot-com bust was a direct result of so many untruths being told that eventually the investors who were being lied to woke up and said, "Okay no more money unless you can prove to us that you have a history of truth, integrity, and honesty." As a result, only those companies that had been grown "organically" with a proven track record, survived, and the venture capitalists stopped funding the "get rich quick" ego based startups with no "soul" and certainly without a code of ethics.

This was Wall Street's "Armagedden" – a perfect example of how the absence of right action is viewed by the Universe – with a karmic display of disgust, dire personal and financial consequences, and massive retribution. All that was missing were the locusts.

Zenlightened Entrepreneurs

The Key Distinctions of Zenlightened Entrepreneurs

Zenlightened entrepreneurs approach life and business from a perspective that is new, fresh, and rather unorthodox. The differences are sometimes subtle, yet significant, and lead to tremendous success. We have talked about Yves Farges, Arran Stepehens, and other zentrepreneurs. What sets them apart from the tens of thousands who strive for the same measure of success in their businesses?

The differences are more like distinctions, and they are more than just fads or interesting tips from self styled gurus who would have you believe that their method, purchased at high prices will bring you the success you so richly deserve. This year, Donald Trump started his own on-line University. Here is an excerpt from his on-line brochure:

> *"If you want to succeed as an entrepreneur without making the typical – and costly beginner mistakes...If you want to work for yourself and never slave for a boss again. If you want to build wealth and achieve true financial security...If you want to achieve extraordinary success one winning business deal at a time...then this is the right program – and now is the right time...so take the next step."*

The next step being enrollment in a $99 program. In three easy steps Trump certified coaches will teach you the Trump Way to organize your business for maximum profitability and efficiency.

I would be willing to lay odds that hundreds of thousands of viewers of *The Apprentice* will sign up, just because it's The Donald. America is media and celebrity driven, and the perception of success, power, and riches, created by The Donald himself may just be smoke and mirrors, illusionary and not entirely real, however people who are desperate enough to chase the dream will buy anything they perceive to be the winning formula. The distinctions we talk about will not be what The Donald is offering, they will be quantum shifts in how you will approach your business, your personal life, and your personal relationships – for the rest of your life.

Researched from the experiences of hundreds of zenlightened entrepreneurs, here are some distinctions that set them apart from others. First, however, the word distinction should be clarified. Nina East, senior member of the School of coaching says,

> *"We are not talking about 'habits' There's really nothing wrong with habits; many can be good ones, instilling discipline to your daily regimen. The problem with attempting to form habits is that it's easy to backslide because they aren't really yours. Just when you are about to decide they are valuable and working, something comes up that throws in a twist and you find yourself returning to the same old habits. A distinction, on the other hand, is neither a habit or a secret, nor even the latest tip of the day. A distinction is often a subtle difference in language, but it brings powerful insight, meaning, and perspective to the situation at hand."*

As you incorporate these key distinctions into your life and business, you will create a key shift in how you think, how you evaluate, and how you approach any situation. You will soon realize that you cannot go back to your old way of thinking again. Your old habits will be in conflict with a new paradigm.

How many times have you have tried to push an 800 pound rock up a hill. Probably once, and that was enough to prove to you it was impossible. That's the same analogy as forcing your business to the top of the mountain. When you are pushing and shoving you are forcing things to go the way you want them to.

Personal power on the other hand, implies a strength that goes beyond what you might be able to exert. You experience personal power when you align your inner energies, beliefs, and emotions with your outer actions. This will propel you forward toward your goals, with much less effort and fewer toes being stepped on.

Some people talk about this as flow, but it is really much more than that. It is a sense of energy and multiple dimensions working in tandem so that with each step you actually move ahead many paces.

Let's talk about accomplishment. It has a certain degree of finality to it. When the goal has been achieved it's over. It's like the effort to complete a task. In many cases you go from a high to a low. Attainment however can best be classified as more of a spiritual experience that can go far beyond both you and your company. It's more meaningful at a higher level. Zenlightened entrepreneurs have said that when they are in an "accomplish" frame of mind, they were able to get a lot done, but the experience didn't allow them to move any closer to a greater vision or sense of purpose. When they shifted to an "attainment" frame of mind, it allowed them to create the life they truly wanted. The fusion of one's personal vision with one's professional mission grounded in activism with a holistic philosophy will hallmark the next 1,000 years.

When was the last time you put into practice *everything* you learned at a conference, every course you took, seminar you registered for, weekend retreat you took part in, or book you read? Until you put into practice what you've learned you've wasted your money and time. Yet so many business owners and entrepreneurs are on the same treadmill. The difference between them and CEO's of large companies is that it's coming out of their pocket rather than the corporate training budget. Conferences used to be a great excuse to escape reality for a few days with people who shared the same mindset. If you had an accomplice it was much easier to escape the break out sessions and head for the hotel cocktail lounge. And then to your amazement you found it chock full of delegates, also participating in the "Great Escape." Zentrepreneurs look at life long learning rather then quick hit seminars to create visions of value.

Zenlightened entrepreneurs who have been able to attain success in their business and their life when interviewed say that they thought of their lives in compartmentalized segments. Within their businesses they had a segmented approach to their services and products. When they integrated their work and their life, they created a new synergy between the two, thus creating that all important zen balance.

Zenlightened entrepreneurs often learned life lessons the hard way. They spend years working hard, only to see their goals slipping away – along with their health and their energy. Often they "hit bottom" before they decided to try it a different way. When they do make the shift to working joyfully, they find themselves thinking, "Is it really this easy?" or "Wow, this is great! I can have fun, make money, and make a difference!"

When I asked Zentrepreneurs whether they required a great deal of structure in their lives in order to attain success in business and in life, they drew an analogy to environments. They said that a certain amount of structure was a good thing, because it allowed you to focus on the tasks at hand to target specific outcomes. Environments go beyond structure. They set up systems of support that enable successful zentrepreneurs to continue making progress effortlessly. The distinction is that environment works for you, while a structure requires you to do the work.

Zenlightened entrepreneurs say this is one of the most important distinctions. When they could transform their structures – or lack of structure – into environmental supports, they were able to consistently move ahead with far less effort.

When you think of those moments in your life when you had a revelation. It may be a moment or may last longer, but it does cause a behavior change. Then there is a paradigm shift, which can be very powerful and life altering. From that point on it has a profound affect on your life at a deep cellular level. These moments, have been commonly referred to as "aha" moments, the shift is so powerful that your life may never be the same again. You might slip back to the "old you," but only briefly when you realize that you can never go back, only forward, or your full potential will not be realized. Zenlightened entrepreneurs are open to these moments all the time.

People who are struggling with their businesses often describe themselves as being "realistic." They tend to see only what's in front of them...what's not working. The truth is that their vision is myopic, which generally makes things worse. If they were to begin to turn what are really just limiting beliefs into "golden nuggets" of possibilities, their perspective would change to one of optimism rather than despair and defeat. But it's more than just a state of mind, it really requires a commitment to looking at what's working and building a belief system out of that. Now, I can tell you that this is all based on spiritual and scientific principles. Researchers have shown that when our focus is on what's working and our vision and passion are in alignment, we actually find creative ways to make things work. Zenlightened entrepreneurs have mastered this distinction.

Zenlightened entrepreneurs, like Arran Stephens and Yves Farges are grounded both in their life and business. If you can honor who you are and where you are in this present moment in life, you are never frustrated. You never want or need anything more.

When most entrepreneurs or business owners want more, which is not unusual, nor is it such a terrible thing, it signals to the universe that you are coming from a place of lack and scarcity rather than abundance. To further magnify the problem, if you are having a bad month, desperation sets in, which as you know immediately projects on to everyone around you. Nothing stifles the company environment faster than a desperate owner.

When you honor where you are and are fully present, loving each moment, knowing that each moment is already full and perfect, regardless of whether you have accomplished or attained, it is tapping in to the power of now. Honoring where you are doesn't discount that you might have dreams and desires, but in really honoring, you activate trust, celebration, and good feelings that allow in more of what you are wanting. What shifts or distinctions are you noticing in yourself already? What will be your next actions toward becoming a Zenlightened Entrepreneur?

Buddha says:
"By day the sun shines, and by night shines the moon. The warrior shines in his armor and the Brahmin in his meditation. But the Buddha shines by day and by night – in the brightness of his glory shines the man who is awake."

5

The Corporate Criminals

Why Good People Do Bad Things

In the past two years we have seen a rise in the number of entrepreneurs and business leaders caught with their hands in the proverbial cookie jar. What makes everyday people commit extraordinary crimes of fraud and deceit?

Bernie Ebbers, the former chief executive of WorldCom, was sentenced to twenty-five years in jail for orchestrating an $11 billion fraud, the biggest in U.S. corporate history, at the once high-flying U.S. telecommunications company. U.S. district Judge Barbara S. Jones said the sentence reflected the gravity of the crime. "Although I know this will probably mean Ebbers will spend the rest of his life in prison, sentencing him to anything less would not reflect the seriousness of the crime." Ebber's sentence is one of the most severe to be handed down for a white-collar crime. Robert Mintz, a lawyer with McCarter & English, called the sentence staggering. "This sends a very chilling message that if you get convicted of these large-scale financial frauds, you're going to be looking at a sentence that a Mafia kingpin or a drug lord would face," he said.

Ebber's sentence came as United States federal prosecutors decided in a further high-profile white collar fraud case not to pursue perjury charges against Richard Scrushy, the former Health South chief executive. Scrushy was acquitted in a multi billion dollar fraud at the health-care company. The decision brings an end to two years of government efforts to hold Scrushy criminally responsible for the fraud. Mr. Scrushy still faces civil charges.

Era of Imperial CEOs Over

What's the mark of a great conman – he's arrogant, cocky, brazen, and he loves his work!

Jennifer Reingold wrote in *Fast Company* in October, 2003 that there is a new era of accountability. Most of the nation's worst-performing bosses have been shown the door.

> *"The death certificates have been signed. The eulogies have been written. The bagpipes have sounded. That's right, folks. The era of the imperial CEO is officially over. Thanks to the humiliating collapse of the fraud-riddled likes of Enron, HEALTHSOUTH, Tyco, and WorldCom, chief executives today are about as respected as, oh, Internet stock analysts."*

Another prominent departure this past year was American Airlines chief Donald Carty, forced out after neglecting to mention the special bonus pool for top executives while he was asking stewardesses and pilots to take massive pay cuts. And this was just the tip of the iceberg. Many CEOs were knocked off their lofty perch for accounting irregularities, manipulation of annual reports, insider trading, and lavish perks, like Dennis Koslowski of Tyco and his $4 million dollar paintings for his $18 million apartment on fifth avenue, (plus another six residences valued at over $30 million, all at shareholder's and employees expense). Bernie Ebbers of WorldCom received a severance package of $1.5 million a year for the rest of his life, plus the use of the WorldCom jet for 30 hours a year, plus numerous other benefits. Keep in mind that Ebbers had already received $44 million in pay, but claimed he didn't understand that WorldCom had defrauded investors of $7 billion.

- In the year 2000 the average CEO earned more in one day than the average worker earned all year. Twenty-five percent of worker earned less than poverty-level wages. 30 million Americans today earn the minimum wage of $5.15.

- Wal-Mart CEO H. Lee Scott, Jr. received more than $17 million in 2001 (total compensation), while employees were suing Wal-Mart for violations of the Fair Labor Standards Act.

- Former Kmart CEO Charles Conaway received nearly $23 million in compensation during his two-year tenure, while 283 stores were closed and 22,000 employees lost their jobs without any severance pay whatsoever when Kmart filed for bankruptcy in 2002.

- The CEOs of twenty-three large companies under investigation by the Securities and Exchange Commission (SEC) and other agencies earned 70 percent more than the average CEO, banking a collective $1.4 billion in two years, while the market value of these twenty -three companies in January 2001 nose-dived by over $500 billion (or about 73 percent) and 160,000 employees were laid off.

- Enron's CEO Kenneth Lay pulled in over $100 million, while 100 executives and energy traders collected more than $300 million-in the year before the company filed for bankruptcy, with a $68 billion loss in market value, the loss of jobs for 5,000 employees, and $800 million lost from their pension funds.

- Between 1990 and 2000, average CEO pay rose 571 percent, (that's roughly 57 percent per year), while average worker pay rose 37 percent.

- The top 1 percent of stock owners hold 47.7 percent of all stocks by value, while the bottom 80 percent of stock owners own just 4.1 percent of total stock holdings.

• If you were poor enough to apply for the earned income tax credit in 2005, your chance of being audited by the Internal Revenue Service was one in forty-seven, if you collected (not earned) more than $100,000 a year, your chance of being audited was one in 208.

Time magazine reported in a survey that the average annual income of the 400 wealthiest taxpayers in 2000 was $174 million, nearly four times what it was in 1992. The percentage of their income paid in federal taxes was twenty-two percent down nearly four percentage points from 1992.

A stunning 78 percent of the CEOs at the worst-performing 20 percent of companies in the S&P 500 have been replaced within the past five years. "The way companies are managed is more by the numbers now," says Chuck Lucier, senior vice-president emeritus at Booz Allen Hamilton. "If an executive doesn't perform today, he gets shot."

Politics and Corporate Crime

Thirty-one corporate criminals gave more than $9 million to the Democratic and Republican parties during the 2002 election cycle, according to a report released by Corporate Crime Reporter.

Corporate criminals gave $7.2 million to Republicans (77 percent) and $2.1 million to Democrats (23 percent), the report found.

The report: "Dirty Money: Corporate Criminal Donations to the Two Major Parties," was released at a press conference in Washington, D.C.

The top five corporate criminal donors, ranked by total amount of contributions to the major political parties in the 2002 election cycle were:

1. Archer Daniels Midland ($1.7 million)
2. Pfizer ($1.1 million)
3. Chevron ($875,400)
4. Northrop Grumman ($741,250)
5. American Airlines ($655,593)

The report checked the political contributions of more than 100 major companies convicted of crimes from 1990 to this year.

"The Republicans and Democrats are awash in dirty money," said Russell Mokhiber, the editor of the Corporate Crime Reporter. "They took in more than $9 million from convicted criminals. Last year, when the heat was up on WorldCom and Enron, politicians from all stripes returned campaign contributions from these two tainted entities or sent them on to charity. The parties should do the same."

Fast Company magazine and in particular the regular online daily dose of First Impression or "Fast Takes" are a forum for some of the world's best journalists with columns relevant to corporate ethics. On Sept. 19, 2005 an example of the 'Big Business-Big Politics' syndrome appeared in my daily e-mail.

Two journalists interviewing two different individuals with the same mission. Daniel Pink spoke to Charles Lewis, a former high profile broadcaster about Wall Street and Washington – strange bedfellows in the rising tide of corporate greed. And Keith H. Hammonds interviewed Eliot Spitzer, the New York Attorney General who has been fighting an uphill battle to uncover the truth on Wall Street and putting people away for their crimes.

Pink says:

> *"There are no guarantees in business and in life. Luck is always a factor, and the dice can roll against you. But that does not change the fact that those who go about their lives and work with the*

passion to create and build in pursuit of self-created goals are the only ones who will find meaning in the end – regardless of whether the dice roll their way. The fact of the matter is that life is short, and we only carry to our graves the inner integrity of our efforts. Only we know how we lived our lives, whether we cut corners, whether we did anything of value – or whether we took the built-to-flip approach to life."

In 1989, Charles Lewis left the world of high-profile broadcast journalism to invent the world of what he calls "public-service journalism." Lewis, who was awarded a Macarthur Fellowship in 1998, founded the Center for Public Integrity in 1990 to pursue investigative projects that the major media were neglecting. During the past 17 years, the center has produced 10 books and more than 100 reports documenting the often-sordid ties between big money and big politics.

When Lewis was asked whether the problem was based on a few bad apples, Lewis's response was:

"Not unless the whole world is your orchard. That's a lot of apples, folks! More companies are restating their earnings now than at any time in U.S. history. And by the way: They have dumped hundreds of millions of dollars into the political process to weaken any laws that might exist to curb the excesses.

You can't look at Wall Street without looking at Washington. They're joined at the hip. Congress and the politicians were the enablers for those scandals. They needed the campaign cash. The corporate executives needed certain favors. Everyone got what they wanted – except, of course, investors and the public. Ninety-six percent of Americans don't contribute to political campaigns at all. The wealthiest elements of this country are sustaining and sponsoring the political process and its actors. What that means is that you get a government that's essentially

*bought and paid for by the powerful interests affected by those
decisions. Sometimes it does feel like we're trying to force people
to drink castor oil. People don't really want to get bad news. But
information is power. Until you find out the truth, you can't dig
yourself out of the mess."*

Lewis was asked who you can trust today to tell us the truth. "It's
a very short list," he says, "Everyone has been discredited. We
have a situation where we don't trust our government or our capitalist system. The level of distrust right now is probably unparalleled since the 1930s."

So how do we build that trust you might ask, well based on Lewis's theories, we need to set tougher standards, and then to everyone's amazement you actually enforce them. There is an urgent
need in America right now for transparency. That should be the
case for all governments in power, but more so in America where
lying has become as commonplace and accepted as McDonalds –
and "we're lovin it!" There needs to be openness and a set of rules.
It's indeed time for zenlightened leadership, in the boardroom,
the oval office and on Capitol Hill.

Hammonds in his article introduces New York Attorney General
Eliot Spitzer as fitting the part of a crusading cop. In May of 2005
his crusade won national notoriety when Merrill Lynch agreed to
pay a $100 million fine to atone for the misleading recommenda-
tions made by its research analysts.

Spitzer's office is still sniffing out conflicts of interest among Wall
Street's analysts and bankers, focusing for the moment on the analysts who are covering failed telecom companies such as World-
Com and on bankers' practice of allotting initial-public-offering
shares to favored clients.

When Hammonds asked Spitzer what kind of financial crimes he
was investigating, Spitzer replied:

with your investments and spending. "Think of your investments and purchasing dollars as votes. Don't just say no, but vote no!"

Buddha says:
"Any wrong or evil a man does
is born in himself and is caused by himself;
and this crushes the foolish man
as a hard stone grinds the weaker stone."

Failure is Not an Option

How tough is it to be honest these days – really tough? As a child you may have been taught that to fib is okay; a "little white lie" has never hurt anybody. How about that little fib when you didn't declare that new suit you bought across the border. They'll never find out, I'll just wear it. Or how about when you made excuses to the teacher when you didn't do your homework. Any excuse to avoid the preconceived notion that the result of the truth would mean a terrible punishment or reprimand – in the mind of an eight-year old, a fate too gruesome to imagine. The fear of discovery is far greater than the unknown consequence of the truth.

As a society we are driven to succeed in virtually everything we live our lives for. In public school, in university, in sports, in our marriages, in our businesses, and in our relationships with our children, everything is measured by success. This need for success is the single most destructive force operating in our free enterprise system. If you doubt this, just look at the self-help section of any bookstore, where shelves are lined with books on "How to Succeed" in everything from business, sales, your marriage and relationships, to your golf game, your tennis game, your poker game, and your life.

It seems every new workshop or seminar has a Tony Robbins look-alike telling you he or she has the seven secrets of highly successful people and for $1000 he'll tell you the secrets so you no longer have to walk around with your head down wondering how you became such a failure. I know the game because I played it. I am a recovering Tony Robbins franchise owner. Many men and women who have risen to the top inwardly feel like imposters. If asked, they may reveal that their biggest fear is being found out. In Robbins' book, *Ultimate Power*, "Fake it till you make it" is his war cry. It's okay to pretend for a while; just never admit that you are afraid, or that you don't know yourself.

Fear of failure corrupts the mind. Because we are programmed to avoid it at any cost, it makes us do things we would not ordinarily do without thought or remorse. Failure is not an option is the mantra of many young entrepreneurs who have just started their new business, while in the background ring the incessant voices of the fallen, the dot-com failures, and the overnight millionaires who have now gone bankrupt and taken tens of thousands of unfortunate believers with them.

Buddha says:
"The wrong action seems sweet to the fool
until the reaction comes and brings pain
and the bitter fruits of wrong deeds
have then to be eaten by the fool."

6

The Pyramid Scheme Epidemic

contributed by Robert L. Fitzpatrick

Robert L. Fitzpatrick, author of *False Profits: Spiritual Deliverance from Multi-Level Marketing*, has done extensive research on this industry and how it is riddled with deceit, trickery, and false promises. Here are his revealing and startling discoveries.

Corruption in Low Places

In recent years it has become quite easy to point out extraordinary corruption in the high places of government and business. Unfortunately this exercise is often accompanied by an assumption that all the rest of us were betrayed, misled, or abused by the privileged and powerful. We are essentially innocent. They are villainous.

I invite you to join me in an inquiry that includes corruption in low places, that is, among all the rest of us. Let us consider that the highly publicized corruption among CEOs has a mirror image in the population at large. Reflecting the documented behavior of the corrupt CEO, we are speaking of unconscionable deception, callous manipulation and an extreme lust for and sense of entitlement to wealth exhibited in the behavior of millions of people, indeed implicating almost all of us. We are speaking of an ethical lapse of unprecedented proportions.

Undeniably, the standards at the top can set a tone for all others below and, to that extent, crimes in the boardroom take on far greater importance than those of ordinary people. In the inquiry we are about to embark upon there are unscrupulous and voracious individuals at the top; however, we will not be able to exonerate the rank-and-file citizenry who are associated with these corporate criminals. Their actions will be shown to aid and abet the predators at the top whom thousands passionately defend and emulate.

In this discussion, we might even turn the conventional analysis of corporate corruption upside down. Rather than the executives corrupting and abusing the public for their own self-aggrandizement, we might try on the possibility that the executives have only tapped into cultural shifts among the public at large and given these shifts a concrete form for rapacious expression. The shameful complicity of government regulators in this analysis, correspondingly, might be seen, not just as abuse of public offices, but as the expected result of paltry public outcry, a hideous reflection of broad public acceptance.

This essay is neither a harsh moral judgment upon modern culture nor a prying inquiry into people's private peccadilloes. Rather, in keeping with the theme of public business and official boardrooms, I am referencing a well-known industry that has exploded in size within the last several decades to a scale of tens of billions of dollars. Each year it attracts as many as five million U.S. residents as investors and participants and a similar proportion in Canada. In the last several years, it has been aggressively exported to Third World nations along with its culture of lying and exploiting. Just as so many North Americans have embraced it, so too are millions in Asia and Latin America.

We are speaking here of the multi-level marketing (MLM) industry, sometimes called network marketing. But these labels and references to it as an "industry" are misnomers. What we are actually talking about are devastating pyramid schemes. The pyramid scheme is a form of mass corruption in which the values and ethics of the classically corrupt CEO are exhibited among millions of ordinary people. As in the boardroom, where privileged position becomes opportunity to loot the company, the pyramid scheme promises each and every participant a chance at being positioned at the "top" and thereby entitled to the investments of those "below." Just as the amoral CEO sees nothing amiss in squeezing salaries and pensions of employees and retirees in order to boost dividends or stock options, the psychology of the pyramid scheme persuades its members that one person's losses are another's gain. The goal is to be the beneficiary of this system, a "winner." And, just as the Boardroom Looters tap into vast resources of the entire enterprise, including customers, investors, pensioners, and suppliers, the pyramid scheme excites similar visions of "unlimited" wealth from an "infinite" chain of recruits in a "downline."

To be more precise, I am describing a worldwide network of companies that exploded in size and reach only in the last twenty years. This group of companies evolved from a legitimate system of multi-tiered direct sales forces that offered goods to the public. It then morphed into a closed system in which the salespeople themselves became their own customers. In this evolved state, which now characterizes nearly the entire "industry," the investments and labors of each newly recruited salesperson become the source of income to those above. The mission of "direct selling" became only a thin façade for a pyramid recruitment scam. This industry now includes hundreds of companies, virtually all modeled upon Amway, the largest and oldest of this type of enterprise. Amway abandoned direct selling several decades ago, and now admits that less than 20 percent of its products are ever sold. Each year, more than 80 percent of all revenues come only from the investments of newly recruited salespeople. These sales people quickly learn that their actual role is not to retail the products to the public but to recruit other salespeople in an endless chain, and they are promised rewards from each level that subsequently joins the scheme. The chain can be infinite in size and therefore, the scheme promises that the potential income is "unlimited."

We are, therefore, speaking of enormous pyramid schemes, operating on a global scale, which in the guise of "network marketing companies" are now largely sanctioned or at least tolerated by government regulators. This view of governments contrasts sharply with the past when such scams were routinely prosecuted as frauds or "unfair and deceptive trade practices."

While untold millions of people have encountered and suffered at the hands of multi-level marketing, I am one of the very few business analysts who has professionally examined its business model, pay plans, financial statements, and contracts; written a book about its ethics, values, and business practices; corresponded with thousands of its adherents and victims; and become qualified to testify as an expert in state and federal courts against its abuses. I have lectured federal and state regulators and most recently led a seminar in Sri Lanka for central banking officials from five Asian nations who were engaged in combating pyramid schemes in their countries. My booklet, *Pyramid Nation*, which reveals how pyramid sales schemes, despite their violation of state and federal law, have become entrenched in the American marketplace, was also translated into Chinese and used by the Chinese government. In 2005, China officially outlawed the multi-level structure of "network marketing" companies in that country while permitting authentic direct selling to the public at large.

An important fact, in keeping with the rest of the chapters in this book, is that multi-level marketing is an American invention. Its spread and consequent harm to millions of people around the world is a direct reflection of our current business and social culture.

So, first, let us unmask the disguises of multi-level marketing to expose the nature and scale of its fraudulence. Then, we can move on quickly to consider the relevant values and ethics and their meaning to larger society.

Enron for the Common Man

All forms of large-scale corruption wear defensive masks, whether it be the "tips" expected by underpaid Mexican police officers, the protection money of Mafia organizations paid by local businesses, the "campaign contributions" in U.S. politics, or the national income derived in Nigeria by the e-mail frauds upon gullible Westerners. Multi-level marketing wears the most effective of all protective colorings in America. It masquerades as legitimate business in a country that reveres free enterprise. It dresses up as a "direct-selling business" emulating the hallowed tradition of the Yankee peddler. It dons the clothing of "independent business owner" in a nation that prides itself on entrepreneurship and rugged individualism.

Additionally, it wears the costume of a business designed to provide extraordinary income opportunity to the masses of people at a time when such opportunities are dwindling due to industry consolidation and advanced market maturity. It even claims to be an "outside the box" system that utilizes different market forces and economic rules than conventional business, a wave of the future, in the age of "paradigm changes." In the costume of "new business model" its promoters can claim exemption from traditional analysis of profit and loss or supply and demand. Critical inquiries or disparaging arguments are cast as efforts of the "establishment" to suppress its revolutionary emergence and to prevent its wondrous benefits from reaching more people. Bearers of such criticism are dismissed as shortsighted, negative thinkers and those who "don't get it". In summary, multi-level marketing masquerades as a new economic savior for the hungry and thirsty masses.

We should pause here to take note of an uncanny resemblance between MLM's disguise as a new and "unique" business model and the trappings of that now infamous company, Enron. Before it was unmasked as a fraud organized by amoral tricksters who had purchased government protection and patronage, Enron was called a financial "miracle." It seemed to float above the normal laws of economics. Its officers were seen as pious and altruistic, motivated not for their own benefit but inspired by the opportunity they were spreading to so many others with their global enterprises and ever rising stock values.

So, while the assertions made here about the multi-level marketing industry may at first sound extreme, consider the reactions that critiques of Enron evoked prior to its demise. A person who stood on a street corner in Houston at that time and proclaimed that Enron was a pyramid scheme, a house of cards doomed to collapse, would have been reasonably viewed as mentally ill, or at least virulently "anti-business." Any disparaging remarks about Enron's righteous executives were immediately classified as slander and calumny, driven by self-serving or deranged motives. Multi-level marketing may be seen as the Enron for the common man, complete with false identity, political protection, and a culture of plunder.

Distractions and Diversions

As in all magic tricks, there are many distractions and diversions (pretty girl, costumes, smoke, loud music, etc.), as well as pseudo-scientific explanations to allow a rather simple-minded manipulation (card up the sleeve, trap door in rear, cable suspended from ceiling, etc.) to occur without the audience realizing it. The multi-level marketing scam that has spread epidemically across America and now most other parts of the world operates similarly.

The main diversions that induce self-deception are the schemes' false promises of income and its deceptive claim to be a "direct -selling" business, based upon simple "door-to door-selling." The income promises include:

1. Opportunity to magically expand earning power. This income potential is described as "infinite" like the limitless recruiting chain it is based upon. A typical presentation shows the potential of one distributor recruiting just five other people that each recruit five and this continues just seven "generations." The result is over 78,000 sales representatives. Commissions on all of their purchases, the promotions claim, will go to that one salesperson at the top who will be YOU!

2. Continuous income without continuous work. Most products are "consumable" goods that people might re-use month after month. Once the initial work of recruiting is achieved, the money keeps rolling in month after month on sales of vitamins, food supplements, skin-care products, long distance phone service and household cleaning products.

3. Possibility of early retirement provided by a continuous, residual income stream from the labors of others in your sales organization. This eliminates the need to work and save all your life.

4. Personal freedom, financial independence as a self-employed person. No more bosses.

5. Time flexibility to set your own work hours. More time with the children, to take vacations, and to do more in life.

6. Security and protection provided by self-sufficiency against corporate downsizing, government cutbacks, inflation, corporate profit taking, increasing requirements for high- tech competency in the job market and job discrimination against older workers.

7. No risk, an opportunity to enter the business for a low initial investment of money.

8. No need for highly specialized skills or higher education in order to succeed. You already have what it takes.

9. No marketing expenses or "cold calls" to strangers are required. Your friends and associates are your first prospects. Your first recruit is as close as your next door neighbor or your own mother in the next room.

These promises have the power to ignite the imagination, inspire hope, fan the flames of discontent with current employment, and to bond the new recruit to the MLM organization with cult-like intensity. The exercise at the very first recruitment session includes inducing the prospects to envision wealth, freedom, and power. To those who buy in, the scheme is soon viewed as the vehicle of personal and financial deliverance; its executives are elevated to godlike status. In this state, few people will engage in due diligence and undertake a careful analysis of the business proposition.

False Identity

The false promises also distract the recruit from seeing the implausibility and fundamental lie about a "direct-selling business." In fact, almost no one in multi-level marketing earns a profit from direct selling to retail customers. The money, as implied in the promises, comes from endless chain recruitment of other salespeople. Though the scheme outwardly resembles a "direct-selling" company, this is a façade, a false identity. Closer examination reveals that the scheme is not structured for direct selling, but for pyramid recruiting.

• The products are overpriced and undifferentiated. Similar or even identical products are available for purchase at lower prices from other companies, in stores or over the Internet.

Since only those with three levels below them are profitable, only the top person and the individuals in levels #1 and #2 qualify. All of the people in the next three levels below do not have enough "downline" to generate a profit. This means that only
31 out of 3,906 or less than one percentage in the six-level chain have as many as three levels below them and are profitable. More than 99 percent are unprofitable based on their position while the one person at the Top profits extravagantly. This basic formula holds true no matter how much further the chain extends. Approximately 99% will be positioned at the bottom of the chain where profit is not possible. A tiny few will benefit, and those who start the scheme benefit handsomely from each new recruit.

The trick of the scheme is to cover up this reality and to convince each and every enrollee that he/she can succeed by building this large and deep downline. Recruits are told that the program is a formula for wealth for all.

A recent study by the consumer group Pyramid Scheme Alert (www.pyramidschemealert.org) of eight major MLM companies revealed that 99% of all sales representatives each year earned less than $14 a week in rebate income. This figure is before all business expenses, inventory purchases, and taxes are deducted. The income amount therefore represents a significant financial loss for virtually all that join these schemes. Additionally, the report shows that no net income was earned on average by MLM distributors from door to door "retail" sales.

The organizers of these schemes know full well of the historical loss rates yet flamboyantly claim these schemes represent the "opportunity of a lifetime."

One further element of MLM's tricky math is the promoters' use of the "infinite" expansion myth. Of course, the schemes cannot expand indefinitely. If they could, at just the thirteenth level of the five-recruit-five-each plan would require more human beings than currently reside on the planet.

In fact, MLM pyramid schemes do not proceed in an unbroken exponentially expanding pattern. They do not even fully or quickly saturate areas with new members. This is because most participants quit within a year. With a 99 percent loss rate among the sales people, all such schemes experience a consequent 50–90 percent annual dropout rate.

When the higher up recruits of the new recruits become discouraged and drop out, the rebuilding process must start yet again. And while the hopefuls engage in this constant rebuilding effort, they are also continuously paying money to the scheme and its organizers for products and training as well as incurring other business expenses. Eventually, they drop out too. Thus, the scheme is continuously luring in new investors, fleecing them, and then replacing them as they eventually drop out in "failure." There is no stable base of sales-people, and there never was a base of retail customers, just a constant churning of financial failures whose losses are transferred to the top as "profits." In this manner, the schemes do not experience sudden "collapse" but rather a continuous process of collapse in which the bottom levels – the vast majority – suffer devastating losses each year.

Lacking government investigation, most schemes can, therefore, go on for many years by successfully recruiting new people to refill the bottom ranks. And as geographic areas finally do become saturated, the schemes move on to new countries and tout their program to new and unwitting people, as the "opportunity of a lifetime." Such is the elusive and tricky nature of the scheme.

The Pyramid Scheme as a Mirror

Chameleon-like, pyramid schemes can take on various superficial forms and public disguises, but the ugly realities below the surface and the inherently destructive values are consistent.

1) Pyramid schemes are about quick, short-term profit.

2) Pyramid schemes require a wanton lack of responsibility toward others. Profit is gained from someone else's loss. The values of the pyramid are those of the scavenger.

3) Deception in the pyramid is pervasive and involves lying to others and lying to oneself. Yet, in the context of their operation, the deception is posed as useful, necessary and ordinary.

4) Inside the pyramid, a kind of looters' mentality takes hold to justify this behavior. If everyone is doing it, why can't I? And, isn't it okay to steal from those who are trying to do the same thing?

5) And, finally, no one who studies pyramid schemes can fail to notice that pyramid schemes are characterized by a kind of lapse in common sense among the adherents. Denial and delusion are in full tilt as visions of riches and freedom are characterized as "positive thinking." Multi-level marketing zealots, who have lost thousands of dollars already, will insist the program is valid and that "success" is just around the corner.

Many will assert that all those who lose bring the losses upon themselves due to laziness, lack of character, or refusal to learn the "secrets" of success. Many gleefully join programs that fleece 90 to 99 percent of all participants – many of them friends, relatives and neighbors. And then, in the instances where the police or the state Attorney General informs them that the scheme is illegal and harmful, thousands deny its harm and defy the government.

In Texas, a large group of women hired lobbyists and tried to pass a state law that would make the most blatant of all pyramid schemes, the so-called gifting clubs, legal. A national business association of MLM companies is currently seeking to get state and federal laws changed to make pyramid recruitment schemes legal in which there is little or no retail selling. Officially, the United State Federal Trade Commission, most state laws, and several federal court rulings classify such schemes as illegal pyramid sales schemes.

Where else in society can we see the pyramid scheme's predatory dynamics of positioning, wealth transfer, and leveraging coupled with this syndrome of deception and delusion? My own evaluation has led me to see the MLM pyramid scheme as very much part of the "mainstream" or, more accurately, the mainstream increasingly resembles the pyramid scheme. Consider:

- The entire NASDAQ bubble, which finally burst in the year 2000, operated on the pyramid model, characterized by the infamous "pump and dump" stock schemes. Stock values based purely on hype and manipulation skyrocketed for those that "got in early." And this mass mania was driven by the nation's top brokerage houses, accounting firms, and respected consultants and analysts.

- Insider trading, which is certainly more prevalent than Martha Stewart's little case, fits the pyramid model. Profit is gained by being in the right place – on the "inside." The level of investments of others on the outside determines value.

- Exorbitant CEO pay is consistent with pyramid structure and values. The massive payoffs are based not on actual contributions or performance, but by being properly positioned at the "top." In 1980, CEOs of large companies on average earned forty-five times as much as non-supervisory workers. By 2000, CEO pay had ballooned to 458 times as much as ordinary workers' at their companies.

- The current mania for stock speculation in general fits the description (including day-trading on the Internet), and now includes millions of ordinary people. We all want a piece of the "action." What action? Quickly earned capital gains on the rise in stock value that is tied to speculation by others that invest "later."

- The widespread use of stock option pay plans for employees and top management had many of the pyramid scheme elements. By paying with options rather than money, the company did not have to record the payment as a cost, but could use the options as tax deductions. This artificially drove up profits, which made the options more valuable and set the stage for the next round of options based on yet a higher price than the one before.

- The reliance of millions of people on investment portfolio or real estate value growth for retirement rather than on continuous savings. Our real estate or stocks are expected to grow at such a rate that frugality is unnecessary. We are banking on there being many more people behind us able and willing to pay more, much more, than we did for our assets. We are leveraging the future buyers.

- Government deficits must be included in this list. In a deficit program, the government borrows billions and spends it on our behalf – now. If the deficits are not paid, we won't be the ones to suffer. We can pass the debt on to the next generation, our "downline," so to speak.

What the MLM pyramid epidemic may indicate is that the values and ethics that we have come to identify with the sociopathic business leader may actually be mirror images of the society at large. Corruption in high echelons of government and business is mimicked in the grassroots. This reality is much harder to accept and will be given less publicity since it is self-incriminating and lacks the news appeal of "villain and victim." Far from an aberration, multi-level marketing may just be the purest and starkest example of what have become the debased but widely held values and ethics of business.

The fact that MLM pyramid scheme participants are part of mainstream America does not in any way lessen the personal and social harm, the financial losses or the corrupting influence. The damage grows proportionately. The losses accumulate exponentially. Moreover, in an era when millions are losing jobs to globalization and new technology, the legalization or general acceptance of business practices designed to fleece unwitting and sometimes desperate consumers of their savings will have long-term negative effects.

Beyond deception, delusion, and desperation, the most important "meaning" of pyramid schemes may be their corruption of the core values and loftiest aspirations of the American people.

7

Corruption in High Places

Is Your Boss a Psychopath?

Zentrepreneurism is about making a fundamental shift in the way North America does business, as well as a swing toward a new era of zenlightened capitalism, where the chief "embezzlement" officer is replaced by the chief "enlightenment officer."

One of the most intriguing notions about business and the corporate corner office came from a most unlikely source. What's really fascinating is that it didn't come from the Wharton School of Business or a conference sponsored by one of the Fortune 500 with a panel of top business experts. It was at a convention of Canadian law enforcement agencies held in the province of Newfoundland. The speaker was seventy-one year old Robert Hare. Hare is professor emeritus at the University of British Columbia, who remains relatively unknown in the business world.

He is however highly respected and renowned in his own field of criminal psychology.

Robert Hare is the creator of the Psychopathy Checklist. The 20-item personality evaluation has exerted enormous influence in its quarter-century history. It's the standard tool for making clinical diagnoses of psychopaths – the one percent of the general population that isn't burdened by conscience.

According to Hare:

> *"Psychopaths have a profound lack of empathy. They use other people callously and remorselessly for their own ends. They seduce victims with a hypnotic charm that masks their true nature as pathological liars, master con artists, and heartless manipulators. Easily bored, they crave constant stimulation, so they seek thrills from real-life "games" they can win – and take pleasure from their power over other people."*

On that day of August in 2002, Hare presented a talk on psychopathy to around 150 police and law enforcement officials. The FBI and the British justice system have long relied on his advice, so he has become somewhat of a legendary figure. He created the P-Scan, a test widely used by police departments to screen new recruits for psychopathy, and his ideas have inspired the testing of firefighters, teachers, and operators of nuclear power plants.

Hare began his presentation that day by talking about Mafia hit men and sex offenders, whose photos were projected on a large screen behind him. But then those images were replaced by pictures of top executives from WorldCom, which had just declared bankruptcy, and Enron, which imploded only months earlier. The securities frauds would eventually lead to long prison sentences for WorldCom CEO Bernard Ebbers and Enron CFO Andrew Fastow.

"These are callous, cold-blooded individuals," Hare said." They don't care that you have thoughts and feelings. They have no sense of guilt or remorse." He talked about the pain and suffering the corporate rogues had inflicted on thousands of people who had lost their jobs or their life's savings. "Some of those victims would succumb to heart attacks or commit suicide," he said.

Then Hare came out with a shattering supposition. He said that the recent corporate scandals could have been prevented if CEOs were screened for psychopathic behavior. "Why wouldn't we want to screen them?" he asked. "We screen police officers, teachers. Why not people who are going to handle billions of dollars?" It's Hare's latest contribution to the public awareness of "corporate psychopathy."

He appeared in the 2003 documentary *The Corporation*, giving authority to the firm's premise that corporations are "sociopathic" (a synonym for "psychopathic") because they ruthlessly seek their own selfish interests, "shareholder value," without regard for the harms they cause to others, such as environmental damage. What if Hare's suppositions are true? Are corporations 'fundamentally psychopathic organizations that attract similarly disposed people? It's a compelling idea, "especially given the recent evidence.

When you look at the previous chapters and the list of corporate criminals, you can easily see what can happen when our business culture becomes malignant. We have long viewed people at the top in key executive positions as powerful, charismatic, visionary and tough. As long as they were delivering bottom line profits and raising share prices, we were willing to overlook that they can also be callous, cunning, manipulative, deceitful, verbally and psychologically abusive, remorseless, exploitative, self-delusional, irresponsible, and megalomaniacal. So we collude in the elevation of leaders who are sadly insensitive to hurting others and society at large.

You would think that by now we would have removed the cancerous tumor from most executive suites. However, in pioneering long term studies of psychopaths in the workplace, an industrial psychologist in New York, Paul Babiak focused on a half-dozen unnamed companies: one was a fast-growing high-tech firm, and the others were large multinationals undergoing dramatic organizational changes, severe downsizing, restructuring, mergers and acquisitions, and joint ventures. That's just the sort of corporate tumult that has increasingly characterized the U.S. business landscape in the last couple of decades.

His theory is that just as wars can produce exciting opportunities for murderous psychopaths to shine, as example, Serbia's Slobodan Milosevic and Radovan Karadzic, Babiak found that these organizational shake-ups created a welcoming environment for the corporate killer. "The psychopath has no difficulty dealing with the consequences of rapid change; in fact, he or she thrives on it," Babiak claims. "Organizational chaos provides both the necessary stimulation for psychopathic thrill seeking and sufficient cover for psychopathic manipulation and abusive behavior."

Take the Quiz

The standard clinical test for psychopathy, Robert Hare's PCL-R evaluates twenty personality traits, but a subset of eight traits defines what he calls the "corporate psychopath" – the non-violent person prone to the "selfish, callous, and remorseless" use of others. Does your boss fit the profile? Do you? Does your board (collectively)? This is a do-it-yourself quiz drawing on the test manual and Hare's book *Without Conscience*. Here are some examples from the quiz:

Is your boss glib and superficially charming?
Does he have a grandiose sense of self-worth?
Is he a pathological liar?
When he harms other people, does he feel a lack of remorse or guilt?
Does he fail to accept responsibility for his own actions?
Is he a con artist or master manipulator?
Is he callous and lacking in empathy?

Top 10 Bosses from Hell

I am asked why am I writing a book called *Zentrepreneurism* and why now? Is the world really ready for a new approach to zenlight-

#5 Harold Geneen

"Perhaps history's most dictatorial accountant, Geneen ran the huge ITT in the 1960s and 1970s. His method: publicly humiliating his top 120 executives every month at grueling, four-day, 14-hour-long meetings that made some of them physically ill. Geneen liked to see the pained expressions on their faces as he tore into them."

#4 Walt Disney

"The man behind the Mouse was a suspicious control freak – a dictatorial boss who underpaid his workers, clashed with labor organizing efforts, made anti-Semitic smears about the other Hollywood studio heads, and wouldn't give due recognition to Mickey's real creator, animator Ub Iwerks, who was supposedly his oldest friend. He also spied prodigiously for J. Edgar Hoover and cooperated with Senator Joseph McCarthy in the 1960s."

#3 Armand Hammer

"Bribed his way through the oil business. Laundered money for Soviet spies. Forced his mistress to alter the way she looked to throw off his wife. Reneged on promises to support his illegitimate daughter. Forced his board members to give him signed resignation letters that he could accept if they ever dared to oppose him. Then promoted himself for the Nobel Peace Prize."

#2 Henry Ford

"Ford used shadowy henchmen to run 'secret police' who spied on employees. He had machine guns, tear gas, and a private army at the ready to deter union organizers. He cheated on his wife with his teenage personal assistant and then had the younger woman marry his chauffeur as a cover."

#1 Al (Chainsaw) Dunlap

"As CEO of Sunbeam in the 1990s, Dunlap charged a bullet-proof vest and a handgun to his expense account. This is understandable given the delight he took in laying off thousands of workers and subjecting his executives to profane and abusive tirades. He threw a chair across the room at his head of human resources, allegedly threatened his first wife with guns and knives, and failed to attend the funerals of either of his parents."

– *Fast Company*, July 2005

Buddha says:
"If a man speaks or acts with an impure mind,
suffering follows him as the wheel of the cart
follows the beast that draws it."

How Do Good People Stay Good?

Or the true story of a zenlightened capitalist.

Carol Newell has been for more than a decade one of Vancouver B.C's most influential citizens, helping to fund ethically "green" charities with an environmental bent, through her personal wealth. She's kept most of her good work under the radar screen, not wanting to have her noble deeds misinterpreted. She decided to give an interview to a local paper, in the hopes that others with fortunes comparable to hers will realize that money is only worth something if it is spent to improve the world.

As one of the family heirs of the small U.S. company that went on to become the Newell Rubbermaid Corporation, the New York-born Newell came into a personal windfall of more than $25 million fifteen years ago, not long after she emigrated to Canada. But instead of spending the money on herself, or using it to amass an even bigger fortune, she has, she says, spent it on building a culture that is "simpler, sustainable for all, and linked to the land." In other words, apart from a modest amount she has set aside to live on, all her money has gone into furthering environmental and social-justice concerns. In six years most of it will be gone.

In 1992, she created the Endswell Foundation, which grants money to charities who are committed to furthering those concerns. She is also working with her business partner Joel Solomon, who incidentally himself is heir to a Tennessee development fortune of $5 million US, in setting up a company called "Renewal Partners." Founded in 1994, it provides venture capital, through loans and/or equity investments, to fledgling companies with a vision for a better British Columbia.

The reality is that eighteen of them have failed, which would be deemed unacceptable by most financial institutions, but this is a risk that Renewal is prepared to take for the sake of their mission. Newell, as we said before, has done this without any publicity or horn blowing. Few people know she even lives in Vancouver. I was renting an apartment in Yaletown, an upscale downtown neighborhood in Vancouver, after a move out of a house. While having a coffee at a nearby restaurant, I noticed a book a young woman was reading and we began to strike up a conversation about life, society, U.S. politics. I told her about the book I was writing and she suggested some people for me to interview. I never saw the woman again, until I read the article in the local paper, and realized it was Carol Newell I had had coffee with.

When Shauna Sylvester received funding from Endswell to start the Institute for Media Policy and Civil Societies, an organization that does communications work for charities, it was two years before she learned who Newell was – or even that she existed. "I didn't know Carol," Sylvester says. "She was an anonymous donor.

In those days, she just wanted her money to be anonymous." Not any more. Newell is now ready to come forward and, she hopes, set an example to other wealthy people interested in seeing their money make a difference.

"I think those of us who have extraordinary wealth have an opportunity to leverage that wealth to stimulate a just and sustainable economy," she told Nicholas Read of *The Vancouver Sun* in her first-ever interview with a daily newspaper. "I know it goes against the grain, but I know it's possible. It's just about deciding what kind of choices we want to make."

What also makes Renewal unique is that when it is considering investing in a new business, the most important criterion on which it bases its decision is not whether the business will make money – though that is important – but how it will contribute to the greater good. "We are about mission and purpose first," confirms Solomon, "and that is unusual." Yes, Renewal wants to see the business plan, he says, but only if it includes a real vision for addressing environmental and social concerns, and if it is going to make a real contribution towards creating a more sustainable and just society.

"We first want to know what the purpose of the enterprise is in addition to creating a successful business," Solomon says. Their website clearly states that money can be provided either in the form of a loan, for which interest is eventually required, or as an equity investment. Terms are negotiated according to the entrepreneur and the type of deal suggested. "The point," says Solomon, "is not to have a prescribed exit strategy. The point is to help these companies remain in business as long as possible." Newell and Solomon have been operating Renewal for twelve years and although committed they are tapped out and not in a position to give out much more.

Newell on the other hand has been busy helping to set up the Tides Canada Foundation, another charitable arm, together with

ness". He says, "Corporate America is stepping in to help shoulder the load. To be sure, their motivation isn't always purely altruistic, but the consumer demands it."

Today's consumers, he says,

"...are wide awake to what's wrong in the world, and they are more inclined to seek solutions. More socially and globally conscious, they tend to avoid companies whom they see as willing to sacrifice the future of humanity on the altar of greed. The new reality is corporations must either align with the expectations of socially sensitive consumers or be left in the dust of their more enlightened competitors. On the other hand, companies that do align themselves with worthy causes and respond to issues affecting their customers are being rewarded at the cash register."

Here are a couple of examples of companies that have turned their cause into cash:

Ben and Jerry's Homemade ANC – Founded by Ben Cohen and Jerry Greenfield and located in Waterbury, Vermont, this company built an $80-million business helping local dairymen by buying milk and cream locally. To meet their sense of social responsibility, they set up the Ben and Jerry Foundation which gives 7.5 percent of pretax profits to nonprofit organizations.

The Body Shop – An $800 million cosmetic company founded by Anita Roddick. The Body Shop has earned a loyal clientele using recyclable packages, refusing to sell products tested on animals and buying materials from underdeveloped areas to improve their standard of living.

It may not be a surprise to find out who is leading the way into this new era of zenlightened capitalism. Zentrepreneurs are on the cutting edge of this economic revolution. Zentrepreneurs are, after all, defined as "zenlightened capitalists." Entrepreneurial minds are creative and resourceful. Of necessity, they must continually look for ways to improve their products, packaging, and presentations. Cause driven to begin with, it's only natural that an entrepreneurial organization would incorporate the concept of philanthropic economics into their business mission.

Dharma and Greed – Popular Buddhism Meets the American

In an exhaustive search for examples of both corporate criminals and zenlightened capitalists, I discovered variations on a theme written by several contributing writers with digital pen in hand eager to expound their own particular theories.

I invite you to think about America, "America, the land of liberty and in the eyes of the rest of the world, the richest nation in the world; America, home of the brave, and equally brave investor. The invitation has been out since the Statue of Liberty was built, inviting all the lost souls to the shores of Ellis Island yearning to be free market capitalists. America, where greed is good, failure is bad, and everyone wants to be millionaire. As a matter of fact, why not have a game show to prove it?

Now I want you to sit in the yoga position and consider Buddhism. Considering Buddhism for many of you might be as painful an exercise as sitting in a yoga position. But consider Buddhism, the Eightfold Path, the road to enlightenment. Even if you have never read a book about Buddhism, or met a Buddhist, your mind might conjure up all sorts of things. Probably you would think of a person in a scarlet robe with a shaved head, which is the most logical, and if you have seen the Dalai Lama on TV, you would imagine him being peaceful and smiling. Now I want you to hold that thought and then think about America again and try to imagine what an American Buddhist might look like, feel, and act like. It's pretty difficult isn't it? Yet American Buddhism – with all its tasty paradoxes fully on view – is clearly an oxymoron to be reckoned with.

Recent estimates have put the number of American Buddhists at somewhere around three million, a group comprising both Asian Buddhist immigrants and Western converts. Often connected to one of the increasing hundreds of Zen centers and other Buddhist training centers in the country, these practitioners range from the traditional monastic adherent (full-time monks and nuns) to a garden-variety working-class Buddhist (or "weekend meditators"), people with houses and cars and families and careers – and a spiritual practice that, while relatively new to America, does have a few thousand years of impressive momentum behind it.

David Templeton, in his book *American Buddhist,* says:

> *"America is a culture obsessed with a hunger for wealth and property, a populace powered by a mainstream encouragement of greed and envy and avaricious desire. Let's face it: in America, if you can't make money, you can't be taken seriously; if you don't dream of becoming rich and famous (or at least rich), you aren't properly American."*

Although Buddha in his teachings taught us that "earthly desires lead to sorrow and pain, that only by transcending greed and envy and the pursuit of material goods will we find true, enduring happiness." Templeton begs the question: "How then does American Buddhism integrate these two apparently opposite ideals? How can you live in a culture where money is necessary, yet follow a spiritual path in which the desire for money is poison? Let's put it another way: can anyone be truly American and truly Buddhist?"

The Dalai Lama posed this question to a gathering of Buddhist leaders in a meeting behind closed doors at a meditation resort in Northern California. They discussed some of the more challenging issues facing American Buddhists at the turn of the century.

"In many ways the Dalai Lama is the perfect symbol of American Buddhism", says Templeton. "As the primary ambassador for the cause of Tibet (the country from which he was exiled after the Communist Chinese invaded in 1951), the Dalai Lama has to walk a tight doctrinal line between serving as defender of Buddhism's basic principles and working as the Tibetan cause's most proficient and successful fundraiser."

> *"Of special concern to the Dalai Lama was the fact there was a growing trend in American Buddhism, especially on both the West and East coast of being attractive to mainly affluent practitioners, those who could probably afford pricey meditation retreats, classes, books, or hand crafted meditation benches. His real question was how to sustain a Buddha mind while living and working in money mad America. His closing message was to emphasize the importance of sticking to the Buddhist basics of the cultivation of compassion and freedom from anger and greed."*

So how does one do that, you might ask? And how does one do that in America?

A Buddhist in America

"It's a problem that a lot of Buddhists in America are dealing with," says Peter Bermudes, director of promotions for Wisdom Publications, a thriving Boston-based publishing company that specializes in books about Buddhism. In a recent article he was quoted as agreeing that "these are major issues for the growing population of American Buddhists." Now twenty-five years old, Wisdom is a non-profit, producing about fifteen books each year. The company's catalogue features more than one hundred titles, from exclusively researched scholarly works such as *Zen Chinese Heritage: The Masters and Their Teachings* (by Petaluma, CA resident Andy Fergusen) to more mainstream reads such as Sandy Boucher's highly anticipated memoir, *Hidden Spring: A Buddhist Woman Confronts Cancer.*

8

Zentrepreneurism

One of my fondest memories is of hosting Canada's first open line radio show dedicated to home office entrepreneurs. The HomeBiz Show was a highlight of my career, and I met some wonderful people along the way. Many of them were on the leading edge, trend-setters and business pioneers. Three of those trend-setters were Mary Meehan, Larry Samuel, and Vickie Abrhamson, authors of the book *Iconoculture – The Future Ain't What It Used to Be – The 40 cultural trends transforming your job, your life, your world* (River Trade Publishing, 1999).

Iconoculture is a marketing firm based in Minneapolis and dedicated to turning future trends into profit. Their homework assignments include reading everything in sight, watching countless hours of television and movies and traveling around the United States to get a feel for what Americans are doing and thinking. Basically, as they put it, they do "what working stiffs would kill for." Wendy's, General Mills and Saatchi & Saatchi Advertising are just a few clients who have turned to Iconoculture to predict the next big thing. The firm also works with Fortune 500 companies, universities, advertising agencies, the media, and individuals.

I interviewed Meehan, Samuel, and Abrahamson in their home office in Minneapolis, Minnesota in 1998, along with their dog Geneva. They had and still do have an uncanny ability to predict trends in our society; most of their predictions made in 1998 have indeed manifested in 2006. The following is a look back and ahead with musings from the book that has relevance to this new world of Zentrepreneurism.

They predicted that the fusion of one's personal vision with one's professional mission, grounded in activism and a holistic philosophy, would hallmark the next 1,000 years. Also, that Zentrepreneurism was surfacing across a wide spectrum of successful, purposeful businesses.

According to the authors:

> *"If you think zentrepreneuring is only for the disenfranchised and old hippies gone to seed, think again. An aging Generation X will carry proudly the do-unto-others-as-you-would-have-them-do-unto-you torch into the future. During their college years, they short-circuit their slacker image by volunteering en masse to help those less fortunate. From coast to ivy-covered coast, college students log as many as ten to twelve hours per week tutoring, manning rape and suicide hotlines, teaching English, serving up dinner at homeless shelters, or being buddies to the physically or mentally challenged. The do-gooding experience coupled with the zentrepreneuristic mood of the millennium will have far-reaching political, social, and economic implications."*

Are the "pick me" Generation Xer's in a mood to become Zenexers and advocates for an enlightened revolution? Time will tell. What we know is that coopetition seems to be replacing competition. People are becoming more interested in work that has purpose, not just a fat salary with stock options and a membership in the old boy's golf club. And companies are forming strategic alliances, synergistic partnerships and mutually rewarding relationships.

More and more employees want to become zenployees, which means they get to participate in decision making, not shoved around like medieval serfs.

In their book they describe a company that has ninety employees, and all ninety employees own the company. Zentrepreneurism in action! It's called the Burley Design Co-op. They build those bright colored buggies, the safety trailers for kids that are behind the parent's bikes.

The Burley Design Co-op is the 21st century enlightened model for building a business in America. "Why would something so simple be the secret to solving the decay of the free enterprise system and the very antidote we need to combat the corruption of capitalism?" the authors ask. "Because everyone wins and nobody loses. How novel a concept where healthy growth is the full time focus of everyone in the workplace."

In a time when thousands are experiencing post-downsizing shock syndrome, this employee-owned co-op structure may be a light at the end of the corporate tunnel. According to general manager Bruce Creps, "There's also a second paycheck that people are after here. Many have tried different things and are looking for meaning to their work."

There is no replacing pride in ownership, which translates into low absenteeism and subsequent low worker turnover, with the inevitable spike in productivity.

One of the principles of the Burely Design Co-op is to enhance the workplace and the community where they live. This little zentrepreneurial company is walking its talk. For sure the Burley team won't be sending jobs overseas to save on labor costs or be forever stressing out over the whims of an all-powerful board of directors, and a greedy, power mongering CEO.

Zenvesting

Here's what Meehan, Samuel, and Abrahamson have to say about investing with a conscience:

"What to do, what to do with that sorry thing you call your life savings....Our best advice: Put your money where your heart is. There are some forty-two mutual funds that invest only in companies that are morally, politically, and environmentally correct. Although these funds typically do not return as well as sinful funds, you will sleep better at night knowing your money is not being invested in tobacco, alcohol, gambling, or military equipment. The Women's Equity Mutual Fund bills itself as one such "pro-conscience" animal. It invests only in public companies that have a proven track record of advancing the social and economic status of women in the workplace. As boomers plan for retirement and inherit gobs of money, expect to see a gazillion special-investment opportunities with a zentrepreneurial twist."

"Who said capitalism and social service make poor bedfellows?" They say:

"On virtually every level of the global economy you bump into the zentrepreneur spirit. Greyhound, that dinosaur of public transportation, is doing great works from which more profitable companies can learn. When Greyhound bought out Trailways in 1987, it inherited the latter's program of offering free transportation home for runaways... Marketers of all shapes, sizes, and colors could explore ventures with alternative trading groups to zentrepreneurize their brands while doing the right thing."

Buddha says:
"Palaces built of earth and stone and wood,
wealthy men endowed with food and dress
and finery, legions of retainers who throng round
the mighty – these are like castles in the air,
like rainbows in the sky, and how deluded
those who think of this as truth."

Zentrepreneurial Spirit

Blending the spiritual with the commercial is a time-honored tradition. Best selling authors like Norman Vincent Peale and Og Mandino have shared their inspiration for decades. Of course, most of that was from a traditional Western perspective. To even the scales, we now have a chance to see how Eastern spirituality can improve our business lives.

Authors Ron Rubin and Stuart Avery Gold, founders of The Republic of Tea, one of the world's finest purveyors of high end tea products, and self-proclaimed "Zentrepreneurs," have written a very motivational book for the aspiring marketer. Loosely blending Zen Buddhism with an American can-do attitude, *Dragon Spirit* manages to be both entertaining and useful.

They say: "First and foremost, believe in what you do, and merely going through the motions of a career simply to pay down your credit card is a waste of everyone's time." Rubin and Gold hammer this point home repeatedly in chapters about passion, perseverance, and faith. "Once you've chosen your bliss, try not to forget even a blissful business needs customers...In building your business, a customer is not someone who buys your idea, product, or service," the authors write, "a customer is someone who becomes part of it."

"While an entrepreneur creates a business, a zentrepreneur creates a business and a life. What we're trying to say is the journey of business and life is an interconnected journey which, in order to attain any level of success, comes down to first discovering what it is that makes you happy. If you're passionate about what you do or what you want to accomplish, the customer base is going to see that, and they're going to naturally drift your way. If you look at what business is supposed to accomplish, and to a certain extent what your life is supposed to accomplish, that is a high level of experience. If you want to be successful at busi-

*ness and marketing your business, it's really about marketing
an experience for the customer and even yourself. It's all about
the experience."*

How many stories passed by your eyes in the 1990s of the dot-
com overnight millionaire entrepreneur. These stories permeated
Silicon Valley. A bunch of fresh faced kids not long out of college
or graduate school wanting to take their big idea or gee-whiz technology to a venture capitalist, in the hopes of getting funding and
spending the next few months building a business.

Their hope? To get a huge payday by taking the company public
or selling it to a bigger company for megabucks. They often got
kicked out of the company, but the millions in the bank account
probably lessened the sting. Here's the story of two opposites –
two zenlightened entrepreneurs.

The New Zentrepreneurs

Despite its location, not far from the dot-com dot-bust Silicon
Valley, in Novato, California, the Republic of Tea has a more enlightened approach to business in contrast to the get-rich quick
entrepreneur.

Rubin and Gold promote a way of doing business that encourages
people to follow their passions and not let work take over their lives.

> *"While an entrepreneur gets hold of an idea, a Zentrepreneur
> lets an idea get hold of them. Essentially, what we're talking
> about here is that entrepreneurs are really about creating some-
> thing because it's going to make a profit."*

> *"Now, a Zentrepreneur does the same thing, only their vision is a
> lot broader. They're doing it and going after it because it's what
> they want to do and that in turn is going to improve how they*

*feel about themselves and about how they're conducting their
own life. You'll find that Zentrepreneurs are the types of people
who are doing it because it's something they can't let go of."*

This makes sense for an entrepreneur, who is in charge of his or
her own company. But how does it also apply to people who work
at big companies?

Well, Rubin and Gold seem to have found the answer at the Republic of Tea:

*"What we tell them is that they're worrying too much about
getting the promotions or recognition. Recognize that you already have been recognized for the job you do. You are the CEO
of You, Inc. or Me, Inc. and everyday, whatever job you're given,
do it in such a way that wows people. It's all about your performance. It's a movie starring you, you're playing the main part
and you have to go in there every day not thinking that you just
have a position in a company. You are the star of the show."*

Zen and Coin or Buddhists in Business

There has been tremendous growth of what we may call Zen commerce in America. More and more Buddhists are in business than
ever before, but why, considering the question of money and its
complicated relationship with American Buddhism.

While all Buddhists must find their own ways to think and act in
regard to money, many practitioners come to Buddhism because
they feel spiritually assaulted when they are in pursuit of mon-
etary gain. Though some drop out of the mainstream completely,
devoting themselves full time to their practice, most merely experience a shift in priorities.

In our fast paced high tech society people are working fifteen
hours a day at their computers, trying to make as much money as

fast as possible. We have talked earlier of the de-humanizing of our society and culture. In Buddhism, people discover the value of moving slower, and they learn that happiness comes from inside them, not from without.

The Sonoma Mountain Zen Center was founded in the mid-1970s, it is financed mainly through private donations and memberships. The center is also creatively generating income through the Zen Dust bookstore and related website. It seems odd to think of a Zen center renting rooms, but most do for the purpose of generating revenues.

The same development of for-profit businesses to support themselves is now commonplace for the modern day Zen centre. One of those is Green Gulch. They operate a very successful organic farm, and a diamond star vegetarian restaurant in San Francisco.

Then there is the Tassajara Zen Mountain Center, above Big Sur, California. It was originally intended to be a private monastery, but has been re-invented as Tassjara, a part-time retreat center.

One of the most impressive examples of zentrepreneurship is the Greyston Bakery in New York City. Founded in 1982 by Roshi Bernard Tetsugen Glassman, its original mission was to support the social outreach programs of the Zen community of New York. Glassman was at one time a system engineer who became a Buddhist monk. His intention was to increase the Zen center's involvement in the troubled, poverty-entrenched region of south Yonkers. Glassman felt that the Greyston Bakery would enjoy large returns by producing pricier fare and decided to specialize in high-end, all natural gourmet desserts and cakes. It was obviously a very good idea. The bakery can now count on regular clients such as Bloomingdale's, Godiva Chocolates, and the White House – and it also provides fudge brownie chips for Ben & Jerry's ice creams.

Greyston now earns close to $3 million a year, motivated by the goal (described in its mission statement) of "feeding poor people by feeding rich people." The majority of Greyston's workers are residents of southwest Yonkers, many of whom were previously viewed as "unemployable." By recruiting its multimillion dollar workforce from the same community the Zen center has been assisting, the bakery represents the perfect example of an enterprise that is both demonstrating a Buddhist philosophy and is clearly a strong money maker, also very American.

Traditionally North American businesses offer assistance to those in need. Large corporations like McDonalds make sizable donations to charitable causes. There is a difference where Greystone is concerned. Their fundamental reason for existence is to profit the poor, while most big businesses like McDonalds exist to profit the shareholders. It becomes a real challenge for a Buddhist to balance the undeniable need for income with the Buddha call for compassion for all people.

It becomes even more of a challenge if the business becomes successful, as there is a temptation to get greedy. This is a spiritual pitfall, for while greed is often perceived as good in America, conversely greed is bad in the eyes of Buddhism.

With the exception of the Greyston Bakery, which appears to be a zentrepreneurial success story, most Buddhist-run businesses try to keep their prices and margins low as a matter of principle.

The fundamental challenge of blending commerce and spirituality is not the exclusive domain of Buddhism, according to Mill Valley, California writer Lewis Richmond, author of *Work as a Spiritual Practice: A Practical Buddhist Approach to Inner Growth and Satisfaction on the Job.*

> *"Right now there's a strong spiritual revival in the Christian and Jewish communities as well as the Buddhist community. And*

guess what? Every religious community is concerned with the spiritual deficits of free-market capitalism, the conflict between compassion and greed. It's a very human problem. Part of us wants to take care of our brothers – and the other part wants to live in Tiburon."

Richmond is a successful software entrepreneur and a former vice president of Smith & Hawken Ltd., the Marin-based gardening specialty outlet. A practicing Buddhist and teacher, he was a founding member of Green Gulch Zen Center, assisting in the development of the center's successful moneymaking enterprises.

"In traditional Buddhist nations," he says, "the teachers offered a clear answer to the problem of money, Buddhists were simply prohibited from touching the stuff. Their original solution was just to stay away from the whole thing and have nothing to do with commerce. So monks have to get donations from wealthy people, and it usually becomes a very corrupt system. But in America, we've developed this ad hoc way of supporting the institution with little money-making schemes," he says. "And I think it's a much better system." Asked if Green Gulch and its affiliates are flirting with the devil, so to speak, by going into business, Richmond responds musingly, "What the Zen centers are running can hardly be called businesses," he says. "A business by definition is an enterprise that produces wealth, which seems to be the predominant activity on the planet. But if you look at these enterprises at Buddhist centers, they are almost all operated with voluntary or semi-voluntary workers. These are non-profit organizations that would never survive as real businesses."

History has proven that when greed is left unchecked it produces harmful repercussions. So what affect does that have on American Buddhists, who adhere to the fundamental precepts of Buddhism, which is to treat all living beings with compassion? Whether you are Buddhist or not, when you start talking about money, is there a compassionate energy around that? You need to ask yourself a fundamental question: is my business enterprise or my job about more than greed? Buddhists will say that the real issue with money is not money, it's the role that money plays in a person's psyche and their life. Zentrepreneurs have a clear understanding of that.

Challenging the assumption that American Buddhism appeals mainly to the affluent is Bob Sweeney, a Santa Rosa, California resident who handles risk issues for an international retail company. He is a twenty-five-year-old practitioner of Nichiren Dai Shonin, a sect of Buddhism in which daily chanting plays a major role. He insists that a survey of his fellow practitioners would result in finding that they cross all economic lines. He prefers not to think of his fellow Buddhists in terms of the amount of money they make. "Society might say that some of us are wealthy and some are not wealthy," he says. "But I see us all as being rich. We're rich in the quality of our lives."

> *"May the poor find wealth,*
> *Those weak with sorrow find joy,*
> *May the forlorn find new hope,*
> *Constant happiness and prosperity.*
>
> *May the frightened cease to be afraid,*
> *And those bound be free,*
> *May the weak find power,*
> *And may their hearts join friendship"*
>
> – The Dalai Lama

9

Social Entrepreneurship

"What business entrepreneurs are to the economy, social entre-preneurs are to social change. They are the driven, creative indi-viduals who question the status quo, exploit new opportunities, refuse to give up, and remake the world for the better."

– David Bornstein, author

Here is social entrepreneurship as defined by the Centre for the Advancement of Social Entrepreneurship at Duke University, or better known as CASE:

"Social entrepreneurship is the process of recognizing and relent-lessly pursuing opportunities to create social value. Social entre-preneurs are innovative, resourceful, and results oriented. They draw upon the best thinking in both the business and non-profit worlds to develop strategies that maximize their social impact. These entrepreneurial leaders operate in all kinds of organiza-tions: large and small; new and old; religious and secular; non-profit, for-profit, and hybrid. These organizations comprise the "social sector."

Peter Drucker introduced the term "social sector" in *Post-Capital-ist Society* when he discussed the need for a sector in addition to the "private sector" of business and the "public sector" of govern-ment to satisfy social needs and provide a meaningful sense of citizenship and community. For our purposes, social sector orga-nizations include any organization whose primary goal is to create value that cannot be reduced to economic wealth for owners or consumption benefits for customers, whether it is related to the promotion of good for human society, animals, or the natural environment.

Here is what social entrepreneurship is NOT as defined by CASE:

"At the same time that social entrepreneurship is gaining in popularity, many business leaders, business schools, and MBA students are increasingly interested in issues surrounding "corporate social responsibility," "sustainable enterprise," "business ethics," or "social impact management." While at times complementary, at Duke, we see these topics as distinct from social entrepreneurship and do not focus on them as part of our primary activities". For a thoughtful discussion of the relationship between social entrepreneurship and social impact management, see Mary Gentile's paper for the Aspen Institute's *Initiative for Social Innovation through Business (ISIB): Social Impact Management and Social Enterprise: Two Sides of the Same Coin or a Totally Different Currency?*

In the non-profit sector, many people also consider social entrepreneurship, or social enterprise, to refer exclusively to income generating non-profit activities, quite often in the form of non-profit business ventures. While the adoption of earned income strategies is certainly a popular trend within the field of social entrepreneurship, and a tool used by many social entrepreneurs, CASE does not espouse this narrow definition of social entrepreneurship and rather focuses more broadly on innovative, resourceful, and opportunity-oriented responses to social issues, problems, and challenges. They see social entrepreneurship not as a specific tool, method or type of program, but rather as an approach to creating social value that embraces the fundamental principles of entrepreneurship.

Social sector leaders span the business, nonprofit, and government worlds. They have diverse passions, goals, roles, and responsibilities. They may be executives, managers, entrepreneurs, board members, philanthropists, or volunteers. Some have spent most of their careers in one sector; others have moved between business, nonprofit, and government jobs. Yet they are united by a common purpose: the pursuit of greater effectiveness and social impact in their social sector endeavors.

The highly regarded Centre for the Advancement of Social Entrepreneurship at Duke University has as its mandate and mission:

"To serve social sector leaders interested in the thoughtful application of business expertise for the improvement of social conditions. We are committed to exploring the adaptation of business concepts, tools and skills to the social sector in appropriate, practical and effective ways."

CASE seeks to promote concrete resources and opportunities for social ventures looking to engage with MBAs and tap into business expertise; for business leaders interested in bringing their business skills to the social sector; and for aspiring social entrepreneurs seeking to connect with like-minded individuals.

Social entrepreneurship is really about applying practical, innovative and sustainable approaches that benefit society in general. The targeted focus generally is around those people who are marginalized and poor. Social entrepreneurs offer unique approaches to economic and social problems by cutting across all sectors and disciplines. Certain values and processes are common to each social entrepreneur, whether their area of focus has been education, health, welfare reform, human rights, workers rights, or environment development. They may also set up either non-profit or for profit entities.

Homeless shelters are starting businesses to train and employ their residents; environmental organizations are partnering with corporations to find economically sound ways to protect natural habitats; and arts groups are exploring new ventures that promise to stabilize revenue and enhance community development. Many philanthropists are increasing their focus on outcomes and strategies for sustainability. Numerous non-profits are adopting the language and tools of business and some are actually converting to for-profit status.

At the same time, for-profit firms are competing directly with non-profits by moving into social sector arenas, ranging from education to economic development to environmental conservation. This rash of sector-blurring activity has created an opportunity for leading business schools to have significant social impact by constructively exploring the adaptation of business concepts, tools, and skills to the social sector in appropriate, practical and effective ways.

By definition, a social entrepreneur's job is to recognize when a part of society is stuck and to provide new ways to get it unstuck. Social entrepreneurs are not content just to give a fish or teach how to fish. They will not rest until they have revolutionized the fishing industry. He or she finds what is not working and solves the problem by changing the system, spreading the solution and persuading entire societies to take new leaps.

Identifying and solving large-scale social problems requires a social entrepreneur because only the entrepreneur has the committed vision and inexhaustible determination to persist until he or she has transformed an entire system. The scholar comes to rest when he expresses an idea. The professional succeeds when she solves a client's problem. The manager calls it quits when he has enabled his organization to succeed. Social entrepreneurs go beyond the immediate problem to fundamentally change communities, societies, and the world.

Ashoka is a global organization that identifies and invests in leading social entrepreneurs – individuals with innovative and practical ideas for solving world problems.

Ashoka's mission is to shape a citizen sector that is entrepreneurial, productive and globally integrated, and to develop the profession of social entrepreneurship around the world. Ashoka identifies and invests in leading social entrepreneurs – extraordinary individuals with unprecedented ideas for change in their communities – supporting them, their ideas and institutions through all phases of their careers. Ashoka Fellows benefit from being part of the global Fellowship for life.

Ashoka Fellow Veronica Khosa was frustrated with the system of health care in South Africa. A nurse by trade, she saw sick people getting sicker, elderly people unable to get to a doctor, and hospitals with empty beds that would not admit patients with HIV. So Khosa started Tateni Home Care Nursing Services and instituted the concept of home care in her country. Beginning with practically nothing, her team took to the streets providing care to people in a way they had never received it – in the comfort and security of their homes. Just years later, the government had adopted her plan and through the recognition of leading health organizations the idea is spreading beyond South Africa. Social entrepreneurs like Khosa redefine their field and go on to solve systemic social problems on a larger scale.

In country after country the number of citizen organizations is up hundreds, often thousands-fold. Tiny Slovakia had a handful of such organizations in 1989 and now boasts more than ten thousand. Of the approximately two million citizen sector organizations working in the United States, 70 percent of them were established in the last 30 years. Eastern Europe has seen more than 100,000 such organizations established in the seven years following the fall of the Berlin Wall.

The revolution – led by leaders like Veronica Khosa – is fundamentally changing the way society organizes itself and the way we approach social problems. These leaders are certainly doing more than giving a fish. They are teaching the world to swim.

The past two decades have seen an extraordinary explosion of zentrepreneurship and competition in the social sector. The social sector has discovered what the business sector learned from the railroad, the stock market and today's digital revolution: that nothing is as powerful as a big new idea – if it is in the hands of a first class zentrepreneur.

A social entrepreneur identifies and solves social problems on a large scale. Just as business entrepreneurs create and transform whole industries, social entrepreneurs act as the change agents for society, seizing opportunities others miss in order to improve systems, invent and disseminate new approaches and advance sustainable solutions that create social value.

Unlike traditional business entrepreneurs, social entrepreneurs primarily seek to generate "social value" rather than profits. And unlike the majority of non-profit organizations, their work is targeted not only towards immediate, small-scale effects, but sweeping, long-term change.

Ashoka says:

> *"Social entrepreneurs identify resources where people only see problems. They view the villagers as the solution, not the passive beneficiary. They begin with the assumption of competence and unleash resources in the communities they're serving."*

What Does it Take to be a Social Entrepreneur?

Jerr Boschee, the President and CEO of the National Center for Social Entrepreneurs, sees the "non-profit mentality" – the belief that capitalism and profits are social evils – as the "single greatest obstacle" in the implementation of entrepreneurial strategies. From experience working with social entrepreneurs, he has come up with what he terms the "raw materials" of social entrepreneurship:

1) Candor
2) Passion
3) Clarity in your mission
4) Commitment
5) Core Values
6) Products and services driven by customers
7) Sound business concepts
8) Willingness to plan
9) Building the right team
10) Having sufficient resources; and
11) Ability to improvise.

Overcoming the nonprofit mentality with these skills is the formula for success for the social entrepreneur.

> *"Identifying and solving large-scale social problems requires a committed person with a vision and determination to persist in the face of daunting odds. Ultimately, social entrepreneurs are driven to produce measurable impact by opening up new pathways for the marginalized and disadvantaged, and unlocking society's full potential to effect social change."*

> *"Social entrepreneurs are not content just to give a fish or teach how to fish. They will not rest until they have revolutionized the fishing industry. This revolution is fundamentally changing the way society organizes itself and the way we approach social problems."*

– Bill Drayton, CEO, chair and Founder of Ashoka

The New Heroes

Corporate scandals and excessive compensation packages for dubious CEOs have dominated business news during the past three years. Profiles of visionary corporate heroes have given way to cautionary tales about greedy villains, and public trust in business has plummeted. At the same time, however, a new kind of business hero, the social entrepreneur, has been gaining media attention and capturing the public's imagination. Even students and faculty in the world's top-ranked business schools – a typically jaded and hard-headed group – are becoming inspired.

Just a decade ago, there were virtually no business school courses or student projects on social entrepreneurship. Today most top business schools have both. Stanford University has introduced the Stanford Social Innovation Review and the Global Entrepreneurship Monitor, a worldwide consortium of academic institutions, chaired by the London Business School. Babson College has just inaugurated a survey to measure social entrepreneurship around the world. But before such a subject can be taught, analyzed, measured, or revered, it must be defined. At the broadest level, a social entrepreneur is one driven by a social mission, a desire to find innovative ways to solve social problems that are not being or cannot be addressed.

With only three employees and a $175,000 annual budget, the International Senior Lawyers Project, a non-profit group that matches experienced U.S. attorneys with needs in developing countries, has dispatched 200 U.S. lawyers across the world in the past four years. They have helped an Indian human-rights law network litigate domestic violence and disability cases. In South Africa, they are teaching black attorneys how to practice business law. And in Bulgaria, they are bolstering public defenders.

In the Manchester neighborhood of Pittsburgh's North Side, Bill Strickland has developed a series of programs to bring new life to the community. At one end of the lifeline is the MCG, whose mission is to rescue at-risk school kids by using the arts to teach them life skills. At the other end is the BTC, a very innovative partnership with local companies to train displaced adults for real work in real jobs. Since their inception, the two programs have each grown into more than $3 million-a-year operations, with a combined staff of 110 people. Strickland serves as president and CEO, the essential element that holds all of the parts together.

Like any true zentrepreneur, Strickland has filled the space between the two programs with other ventures: a jazz concert hall and an innovative Grammy Award-winning record label. Next year, he plans to launch the Denali Initiative, a national three-year effort funded by the Kaufmann Foundation to teach non-profit leaders how to think like entrepreneurs. "You start with the perception that the world is an unlimited opportunity," Strickland says. "Then the question becomes, 'How are we going to rebuild the planet?'"

"Artists are by nature entrepreneurs, they're just not called that," Strickland says. "They have the ability to visualize something that doesn't exist, to look at a canvas and see a painting. Entrepreneurs do that. That's what makes them different from business people. Business people are essentially administrators. Entrepreneurs are by definition visionaries. Entrepreneurs and artists are interchangeable in many ways. The hip companies know that."

There's one other thing about this unique zentrepreneur. Bill Strickland isn't in this for the money. But he's also not into being a starving artist. Strickland is looking for something in-between, like his hybrid model of social entrepreneurship. In fact, he's striving for the one thing that he thinks is missing in the world today: balance. A balance of resources, equity, and opportunity, a socially responsible mind-set that asks the "haves" in this country, "How much is enough?" The world doesn't disappear just because you close your eyes.

The story of Susan Standfield, a new zentrepreneur hero, is just one of many. The encouraging part is she's in her late thirties, so has plenty of time to carry the positive messages about social entrepreneurism. Here are excerpts of her story, as told to reporter Yvonne Zacharias of *The Vancouver Sun* in Sept., 2005.

There is a saying in Africa – moja moja – that translates into English as "one at a time". Susan Standfield has to remember it at times. Through tiny steps and tiny stitches, she is hoping to take bits of thread, swaths of cloth, the rhythms of Africa, the spirit of its children and weave a dream into reality. It all began about four years ago in the middle of the night when she decided she was through with her job in television advertising.

"I didn't like the schedule. I didn't like the pressure. I didn't like how it treated people," said the thirty-seven-year-old Vancouver woman. "It was fine when I was younger. I didn't own anything at the end of the day. We made lots of money but I was always unemployed as soon as the job was over. I thought, I have to build something for my future." She says she hired a business coach to help her find her way. Focus on the things you love, she was advised. Those happened to be four things: kids, photos, Africa and fashion design.

Out of her passion a small company emerged called the Children's Photographic Gallery of Kenya. The company's premise is simple: children in Kenyan orphanages take photos of themselves to be distributed, primarily on T-shirts, for sale. The children are paid ten per cent of the proceeds for their work, raising much-needed funds for the dirt-poor orphanages. In the western world there are many skeptics of this process. A for-profit company helping orphans? Aren't there enough designer T-shirts on the market already? How can this work?

Yet, in Kenyan eyes, there are no skeptics, only hope for possibilities. Standfield initially approached the idea with trepidation. As soon as the words were out of her mouth to the coach, she was terrified. "I thought, oh my God, okay, when you tell somebody your dream, you are kind of on the hook."

She asked herself where to begin with such a dream. Of course, it wasn't the sort of job you look for in the help wanted section of the paper.

She got her answer in an article in March of last year in *The Vancouver Sun's* travel section. North Vancouver freelancer Tim Morrison told readers about coming across a very special orphanage called SHERP, which stands for Samburu Handicap Education and Rehabilitation Program, while traveling in Kenya. Morrison wrote about a heroic and compassionate local woman named Grace Seneiya, who founded the orphanage for children with disabilities in 1999.

Standfield says both she and her business coach were drawn to Morrison's article, which included an e-mail address for contacting Seneiya. It was an "aha" moment for Standfield. She contacted Grace Seneiya and her journey of self discovery began.

Standfield registered the business and then, in July of last year, sent off six plastic cameras to Seneiya along with how-to-photograph instructions with translations in Swahili and examples of the types of photos she wanted. She marked them "for handicapped kids," hoping that would prevent them from being robbed in the mail.

Seneiya admitted to being a bit nervous when she opened the package at the orphanage. She quickly overcame her reservations. "I never thought it would work out because the children had never handled cameras before. But they learned so fast. It only took two weeks to teach them. They were so excited," she said in an interview from Kenya.

Seneiya's faith in the idea brought a gust of fresh air to Standfield, keeping her dream airborne.

Although the Purpose Prize is focused on social entrepreneurs, the awards won't be limited to non-profit enterprises that require grants and donations to survive.

Paul Newman is an example of a social entrepreneur with a self-sustaining enterprise. He has donated $175 million from his Newman's Own Inc. products to hundreds of charities. Another celebrity example is Lee Iacocca's post-Chrysler work developing electric bicycles as a way to cut emissions and take better care of the environment. Prize organizers hope that people will realize that you don't have to be a celebrity to think big and in an entrepreneurial way about social contribution after midlife. The money comes from $9 million donated by the Atlantic Philanthropies and the John Templeton Foundation for the prize's first three years.

Journalist David Bornstein (*The Price of a Dream: The Story of the Grameen Bank*) profiled nine indomitable champions of social change who developed innovative ways to address needs they saw around them in places as distinct as Bombay, India; Rio de Janeiro, Brazil; and inner-city Washington, D.C. As these nine grew influential when their ingenious ideas proved ever more widely successful, they came to the attention of Ashoka, an organization that sponsors a fellows program to foster social innovation by finding so-called social entrepreneurs to support.

As Bornstein interviewed these and many other Ashoka fellows, he saw patterns in the ways they fought to solve their specifically local problems. To demonstrate the commonality among experiences as diverse as a Hungarian mother striving to provide a fuller life for her handicapped son and a South African nurse starting a home-care system for AIDS patients, he presented useful unifying summaries of "four practices of innovative organizations" and "six qualities of successful social entrepreneurs."

Bornstein implies that his subjects are "in the tradition of Florence Nightingale and Gandhi". The inspiring portraits that emerge from his in-depth reporting on the environments in which in-dividual programs evolved (whether in politically teeming India or amid the expansive grasslands of Brazil) certainly show these unstoppable entrepreneurs as extraordinarily savvy community development experts. In adding up the vast number of current non-governmental organizations and their corps of agents of positive change, without a doubt, the past twenty years have pro-duced more social entrepreneurs than terrorists."

Educating Social Entrepreneurs

More and more colleges and universities are offering programs or courses that focus on social entrepreneurship. The ability to com-bine business with social purpose has become attractive to many students. Professor Jon Goodman, director of the entrepreneurial program at the University of Southern California's School of Busi-ness, reports that students with social interests are serious about their work: "The students I see are not laid back or lowering their expectations. Many have a real need to engage in something they consider meaningful."

Often, students pursuing social entrepreneurship may not be con-sidered typical. Instead, they may be activists or community-based organizers on a mission to actualize their zentrepreneurial dream. For example, Robbie Pentecost is a nun getting her business degree at St. Louis University. Her business plan for a restaurant, run by a Catholic charity, would employ mentally-ill homeless people, give them on-the-job training and also bring in revenue for the charity itself. Upon completing the MBA program, Pentecost plans to seek corporate funding to actualize her community-based plans.

Her course, entitled Entrepreneurship in the Social Sector, in-volves living cases of social entrepreneurship to achieve three primary objectives: 1) to understand the challenges and rewards of social entrepreneurship; 2) to build knowledge and skills to respond to challenges creatively; and 3) to learn of the different organizational forms that social entrepreneurship can come in.

"The boundaries between business, government, and the nonprofit sector are shifting as societies search for better ways to provide socially important goods and to solve social problems. This reinvention of the social sector is creating a variety of entrepreneurial opportunities for those who can find creative and efficient ways for private organizations to contribute to the social good."

– Prof. Jon Goodman

Resources for the Social Entrepreneur

Ashoka: Innovators for the Public is a foundation that promotes social change by finding and funding social entrepreneurs. As of 1998 and after seventeen years in business, Ashoka has funded 180 social entrepreneurs working on education and children's issues, 147 working on the environment, 104 on income generation and poverty alleviation, 101 on women's issues and 53 on disability.

Echoing Green is a foundation based in New York that "applies a venture capital approach to philanthropy," providing seed money and technical support to social entrepreneurs. Emphasizing start-up projects, Echoing Green has funded 250 social entrepreneurs worldwide in education, arts, health, and human/civil rights. The process is a competitive one: only 10 percent of the applicants receive funding. Resources on the foundation's website include a newsletter that presents the Fellows' projects and other publications related to organizational development, finances, personnel, and public relations.

The Roberts Enterprise Development Fund (REDF), a project of the Roberts Foundation in the San Francisco area, was created to "expand economic opportunity for homeless and very low-income individuals through the creation of social purpose business ventures." The REDF provides multi-year funding to social entrepreneurs and access to business technical assistance from MBA interns. Currently, the REDF supports eight non-profit organizations that are operating twenty-five business ventures. More information can be found, including a downloadable form of the book, *New Social Entrepreneurs: The Success, Challenge and Lessons of Non-Profit Enterprise Creation*, at their website, located at www. redf.org.

which are using increasingly sophisticated market analyses to show corporate managers (and fellow shareholders) the wisdom of following a voluntary course of action in areas of potential social criticism.

Mongoven says that

> *"Shareholder activism is poised to emerge as a central policy-making vehicle for three reasons. First, there is the deregulatory political culture that dominates federal policy-making. A second element is growing economic globalization – coupled with the removal of trade barriers – which has led to recognition of the important role (positive and negative) that corporations can play in developing countries. The third major reason is the increasing accountability and transparency demanded by shareholders and required by securities regulators in the wake of the corporate scandals of the 1990s. All three of these trends continue to domi-nate new regulatory policy-making in the United States. Of the three,* **shareholder activism** *is emerging as the most powerful avenue for changing corporate policy over the long term."*

This strategy is most visible in the climate change debate, where a number of corporations, including many energy companies, have adopted climate change policies as a result of shareholder pres-sure. No action is likely at the federal level on climate change for at least a couple of years. Many influential shareholder activists argue that regulation is inevitable and that, consequently, com-panies should begin to change their internal mechanisms now in order to prepare for dramatic regulatory changes and potential liability.

One of the best arguments for shareholder campaigns is that the ethics and mores of our society are going through rapid change. Those corporations who respond quickly to these changes will move to the front of the line in the public's eye. If they adjust their policies before they feel the thrust of changing values, management and shareholders alike will not only be patting themselves on the back, but feeling good in the process.

The use of child labor in developing countries, for instance, recently was accepted practice in certain industries, but now allegations of child labor represent significant risk to corporate brands – just ask Nike or Kathy Lee Gifford. Similarly, it was once acceptable for multinational construction companies to build large infrastructure projects that required relocation of significant numbers of indigenous people in developing countries. Incredibly, these projects actually had World Bank funding, however, now the bank won't fund such projects, and corporate executives are becoming more wary of these proposals.

A recent report by Merrill Lynch suggests that

> *"Nike's image has never completely recovered from the allegations that it used child labor, even though it is now one of the most transparent companies in the world when it comes to its supply chain. Shell Oil continues to spend millions of dollars to rebuild its reputation after controversies in the late 1990s. Interestingly, the cost to Shell is best measured in recruiting difficulties. New graduates, particularly in Europe, prefer not to work for a company embroiled in human rights or environmental controversies. Socially responsible shareholder groups are increasingly successful in bringing this same argument to mainstream investors."*

As time progresses in this new era of "zenlightened" capitalism, the lines of communication and credibility will be strengthened between the socially responsible investment community and the mainstream investment community. There will be an acceptable acceleration of activist activity and they will be able to expand their demands even further, leaving their mark in the new world of doing business, and Zentrepreneurism will become a corporate model for the 21st century.

Corporate Karma

"Bad things happen to every company, even the best companies," says Paul Godfrey, an associate professor of strategy in BYU's Marriott School of Management. "And just like a business with fire insurance is more valuable than one without it, businesses that have earned a reputation for being generous through acts of philanthropy are given the benefit of the doubt when negative events occur." When accidents happen, lawsuits are filed, or harmful news coverage creeps out, shareholders, customers, and industry regulators often question if managers are looking out for anyone but themselves," says Godfrey. "If a company has demonstrated its character through philanthropic giving and community outreach efforts, such criticism may be tempered."

"The stock price will rebound more quickly, management won't be viewed as harshly, fines will be less, boycotts may be shorter," says Godfrey, "and to a shareholder, that's valuable." Intangible relationship-based assets, which can be worth millions to a company and its shareholders, are often the very assets that receive the most benefit from philanthropic efforts in the event of misfortune," he says. "Part of the reason that people have had such a hard time seeing the justification for corporate giving is that they don't see any extra revenue being generated from the expense." says Godfrey. "What I argue in my paper is that they should look at it more like reputation insurance." Jeffrey S. Harrison, the W. David Robbins chair in strategic management at the University of Richmond, said Godfrey's article provides compelling economic justification for corporate giving.

"In this regard, it is truly groundbreaking research," said Harrison. "For many years scholars have debated whether there is any sound economic justification for corporate philanthropy. Godfrey's well-grounded explanation that 'doing good' provides insurance-like protection for companies because of the goodwill it creates is very significant. I am sure it will promote a lot of additional inquiry."

Along with the economic incentive his model gives to managers to allocate a firm's resources toward philanthropy, Godfrey suggests that companies can still think of ways giving can be directed to further business interests. "For example, it would make sense for an outdoor outfitter like REI to make donations to organizations that promote nature or trail conservation," says Godfrey. "Or, in the case of Qwest, a telecommunications company with a broad range of customers, the strategy might be to give to promote education or literacy, interests that are somewhat related to communication and that would appeal to the company's diverse customer base. That way, consumers see that the companies they frequent are concerned with the same issues that are important to them. Consistency in giving is important to building the reputation that help companies weather storms."

"Just like an insurance policy has premiums that must be paid to keep them current, a company can't expect to give one time and receive any coverage. This is something a company has to work at, but it works because philanthropic activity is morally discretionary rather than obligatory."

Buddha says:
"The fair tree of Void abounds with flowers, acts of compassion of many kinds, and fruits for others appearing spontaneously, for this joy has no actual thought of another."

Socially Responsible Investing

The following is a list of social investment websites:

Calvert Social Investment Foundation:
www.calvertfoundation.org
Calvert Foundation offers a professionally managed investment

note that individuals and institutions utilize to finance local community programs. Its activities fund affordable housing, microcredit and non-profit social enterprises across the country and around the world, creating jobs, building homes, and changing lives through your investments.

Green Money Journal:
www.greenmoney.com
A bi-monthly newsletter with twenty-four pages featuring socially and environmentally responsible investing (SRI) business and consumer resources. The website contains all the articles in the newsletter plus much more. Links to other socially and environmentally responsible companies and organizations are included.

Investors' Circle:
www.investorscircle.net
A non-profit national network of angel and institutional investors, foundation officers, and entrepreneurs who seek to balance financial, social, and environmental returns. IC is dedicated to catalyzing the flow of capital to private companies that deliver commercial solutions to social and environmental problems. Each year IC sponsors venture fairs and a national conference, in addition to circulating deal flow to its members. Since 1992, Investors' Circle has facilitated the investment of over $80 million in 120 socially responsible companies and small venture funds. Behind each of these investments is the belief that business – not government or philanthropy – must lead the transition to a sustainable economy.

Social Investment Forum:
www.socialinvest.org
A national non-profit membership association dedicated to promoting the concept and practice of socially and environmentally responsible investing. Comprising more than six hundred financial professionals and institutions, including financial professionals, institutions, researchers, foundations, community development organizations, and public educators. Membership

is open to any organization or practitioner who wishes to partici-pate in the socially responsible investing field. Member benefits include networking opportunities, information and advocacy.

Trillium Asset Management:
www.trilliuminvest.com
For over twenty years, Trillium Asset Management Corporation has been a leader in socially responsible investing. Trillium is an employee-owned firm, guided by a belief that investing can return a solid competitive profit to the investor while also pro-moting social and economic justice. Its professional staff, in four offices across the U.S., carries on a mission begun in 1982: to help clients meet their financial goals and have a positive impact on society through socially responsible investing. Trillium Asset Management manages investment portfolios for a broad array of individuals and institutions, including high net worth families, foundations, churches, endowments, and the entertainment industry.

11

The New Era of Zenlightened Capitalism

For decades, environmentalists have been warning us that human economic activity is exceeding the planet's limits. Of course we keep pushing those limits back with clever new technologies; yet living systems are undeniably in decline.

"These trends need not be in conflict, in fact, there are fortunes to be made in reconciling them," according to authors Paul Hawken, and Amory & L. Hunter Lovins in their book *Natural Capitalism: Crossing the Next Industrial Revolution*. This is the first book that I have seen that explores the lucrative opportunities for businesses in an era that is approaching environmental limits.

In this groundbreaking blueprint for a new economy, three leading business visionaries explain how the world is on the verge of a new industrial revolution – one that promises to transform our fundamental notions about commerce and its role in shaping our future. *Natural Capitalism* describes a future in which business and environmental interests increasingly overlap, and in which businesses can better satisfy their customers' needs, increase profits, and help solve environmental problems all at the same time.

According to the authors:

> "Natural capital refers to the natural resources and ecosystem services that make possible all economic activity, indeed all life.

These services are of immense economic value; some are literally priceless, since they have no known substitutes. Yet current business practices typically fail to take into account the value of these assets – which is rising with their scarcity. As a result, natural capital is being degraded and liquidated by the wasteful use of such resources as energy, materials, water, fiber, and topsoil.

The first of natural capitalism's four interlinked principles, therefore, is radically increased resource productivity. Implementing just this first principle can significantly improve a firm's bottom line, and can also help finance the other three. They are: redesigning industry on biological models with closed loops and zero waste; shifting from the sale of goods (for example, light bulbs) to the provision of services (illumination); and reinvesting in the natural capital that is the basis of future prosperity."

Citing hundreds of compelling stories from a wide array of sectors, *Natural Capitalism* shows how these four changes will enable businesses to act as if natural capital were being properly valued, without waiting for consensus on what that value should be. Even today, when natural capital is hardly accounted for on corporate balance sheets, these four principles are so profitable that firms adopting them can gain striking competitive advantage – as early adopters are already doing. These innovators are also discovering that by downsizing their unproductive tons, gallons, and kilowatt-hours they can keep more people, who will foster the innovation that drives future improvement.

Natural Capitalism's preface states:

"Although [this] is a book abounding in solutions, it is not about 'fixes.' Nor is it a how-to manual. It is a portrayal of opportunities that if captured will lead to no less than a transformation of commerce and of all societal institutions. Natural capitalism maps the general direction of a journey that requires overturning long-held assumptions, even questioning what we value and how

*we are to live. Yet the early stages in the decades-long odyssey
are turning out to release extraordinary benefits. Among these
are what business innovator Peter Senge calls 'hidden reserves
within the enterprise' – 'lost energy,' trapped in stale employee
and customer relationships, that can be channeled into success
for both today's shareholders and future generations. All three of
us have witnessed this excitement and enhanced total factor productivity in many of the businesses we have counseled. It is real;
it is replicable."*

The next Industrial Revolution has already started. *Natural Capitalism* will prepare you to be a part of it.

During the Industrial Revolution people were vastly more productive because there was low per-capita and a scarcity of people and
an abundance of natural capital. Today we have an abundance of
people and labor saving machines but diminishing natural capital.

Already emerging is the next Industrial Revolution, so what does
it look like? I'm sure you recognize it. It's a not just simply a knee-
jerk reaction to scarcity. It is transforming industrial processes
and business practices to economize on what is now the harsh reality of the most limiting factor of production: natural capital.

*"Companies that adopt these principles will do very well, while
those that do not won't be a problem, since ultimately they won't
be around."*

– Edgar Woolard, former Chair of DuPont.

Zenlightened Capitalists

Panel discussions on "Preserving and Restoring the Commons,"
presentations by the founder of the country's leading brand of
natural household products David Robinson, the son of baseball

great Jackie Robinson, and a venture fair were among the features of the Investors' Circle (IC) 2005 National Conference, which took place November, 2005 in Boston.

The conference, which was based on the theme, "Patient Capital for a Sustainable Future," celebrated the investment of $100 million through the IC network. In collaboration with the popular PBS radio show, e-town, speakers at workshops discussed the state of double-bottom-line investing and enterprise creation in the context of community development, food and organics, health, media, mission-related investing and renewable energy.

Keynote speakers included Jeffrey Hollender, CEO of Seventh Generation of Burlington, Vt., and David Robinson, Director of Marketing for the Mshikamano Farmers' Group in Tanzania. In addition to founding his successful household products company, Hollender is the founder of Network for Learning, an adult education program and audio publishing company, and author of *How to Make the World a Better Place: A Guide for Doing Good.*

Robinson formed United Harlem Growth Inc., a self-help housing development and renovation company, then moved to Tanzania in the 1980s and started a 29,000-tree coffee farm. He helped form the Mshikamano Farmer's Group, a cooperative of coffee farmers, and serves as its Director of Marketing.

Thirty-four companies were featured in a venture fair and two panels discussed the use of private capital and networks to enhance bioregional, cultural, and economic health and diversity. The Investors' Circle National Conference and Venture Fair is the premier meeting place for angel investors, professional venture capitalists, philanthropic investors and entrepreneurs who are using private capital to promote the transition to a sustainable future.

Founded in 1992, IC has become one of the nation's largest investor networks, and the only one devoted specifically to sustainability. Its members and active affiliates are high net worth individuals, professional venture capitalists, family offices and foundations. In its first decade, network members invested over $100 million into 160 early stage private companies and venture funds working to deliver commercial solutions to social and environmental problems.

What is Good Performance to Zenlightened Capitalism?

Every year *Business Ethics* magazine publishes its list of the 100 Best Corporate Citizens. Each year the list becomes closer in alignment with what I have been referring to as a new era of zenlightened capitalism. Here are some of the winners of 2005.

One of the most impressive showings over time has been Green Mountain Coffee Roasters (No. 2) of Waterbury, Vt., a pioneer in helping struggling coffee growers by paying them fair trade prices. The company also supports micro-loans to coffee-growing families, and to underwrite business ventures that diversify agricultural economies.

Xerox also wins kudos on the diversity front from organizations such as the National Association for Female Executives (NAFE), which placed Xerox No. 8 in its ranking of companies based on treatment of female executives. "Women make up approximately a third of their work force; and their number of women managers matches that, with many of those women exercising profit-and-loss responsibility," said NAFE president Betty Spence. "They are a stand-out."

Also noteworthy in the top ten is San Francisco-based Wells Fargo & Co. (No. 6), which donated over $93 million in 2004 to 15,000 different organizations. Intriguingly, Wells Fargo ranked higher than any other company in the category of human rights. It helped finance the construction of affordable single-family homes on or near Native American reservations in seven states, bringing private mortgage capital to those that were historically denied access. No other bank has as many retail locations on Native American reservations.

Wells Fargo's commitment to diversity has deep roots. "We were serving immigrants such as the Chinese right after the gold rush," said Pat Callahan, executive vice president for human resources. "Now we have a separate Border Banking group set up to meet the special needs of customers of Mexican origin."

Cummins, Inc., the Columbus, Indiana-based engine maker has been on the 100 Best Corporate Citizens list all six years, debuting at the No. 62 slot in 2000. Its mission is "Making people's lives better by unleashing the power of Cummins" – a power that comes from 24,000 employees, who enjoy perks like employee ownership and profit-sharing. "A company's top stakeholder is its own employees," a company spokesperson emphasized. "If they are worried about pay or working conditions, how are they going to take care of customers?"

This is a company, you might say, that is firing on all cylinders. It publishes a sustainability report, underwrites the development of schools in China and India, is purchasing biodiverse forest land in Mexico, and funds great architecture in its local community. Its commitment to excellence embraces stockholders, employees, the community, and the environment. That makes Cummins a compelling example of good corporate citizenship.

The 2006 Annual Awards featured:

Starbucks Coffee Company
Corporate Responsibility Management Award
For leadership and excellence in best practices in the field of corporate responsibility.

Patagonia Inc.
Environmental Sustainability Award
For its unique commitment to developing sustainable business practices.

Berrett-Koehler Publishers
Stakeholder Accountability Award
For its focus on creating quality product in collaboration with employees, business partners and customers.

Hypertherm Inc.
General Excellence Award
For workplace innovation focusing on development of people and products.

New to the List in 2006

The list saw quite a bit of turnover from 2005, with 33 companies appearing for the first time. Newcomer Johnson & Johnson (No. 12) receives particularly high marks in diversity. In September 2005, it was one of 101 companies to receive a perfect score on the Corporate Equality Index released by the Human Rights Campaign, which rates companies on factors relating to gay, lesbian, bisexual, and transgender issues.

Also new in 2006 was McGraw-Hill (No. 57), which scores high in diversity, with women accounting for more than 40 percent of managers. Newcomer Milwaukee-based Johnson Controls (No. 73) rates with high marks because of products that help conserve energy. Through the "Buildings for a Livable Future" initiative, the company offers seminars designed to increase customer awareness of the positive environmental and financial impact of green buildings. The company's Brengel Technology Center in Milwaukee was one of the first 12 buildings certified by the Leadership in Energy and Environment Design (LEED) program.

Boise, Idaho-based semiconductor maker Micron Technology (No. 82), also new to the list, wins plaudits for its innovative employee compensation plan, which CEO Steven Appleton instituted in part to avoid layoffs. Employees accept lower base pay than at similar companies, but share in a quarterly profit-sharing cash bonus of 10 percent of after-tax profits. With a limited fixed payroll, the company can theoretically limit layoffs in bad times, while employees benefit substantially during good times. Among other newcomers were Office Depot (No. 45), United Parcel Service (No. 48), Student Loan Corp. (No. 52), and Citigroup (No. 62).

The Top Ten in 2007 were:

1. Green Mountain Coffee Roasters Inc.
2. Advanced Micro Devices, Inc.
3. Nike, Inc.
4. Motorola, Inc.
5. Intel Corporation
6. International Business Machines Corporation
7. Agilent Technologies Inc.
8. Timberland Company (The)
9. Starbucks Corporation
10. General Mills Incorporated

The Eden Project

Tim Smit is the co-founder and chief executive of the Eden Project, located in St. Austell, Cornwall, England.

Smit is an archaeologist turned musician turned botanist who is planting the seeds of change at the Eden Project – his awe-inspiring, $120 million facility in Eden is the world's largest greenhouse, containing 250,000 plants in two giant, enclosed biomes.

But Eden is about more than watching a garden grow. Smit believes that over the next 20 years, in-depth research on plants will result in new materials of unprecedented strength and flexibility, new sources of food and medicine, and new approaches to renewable energy. "We are on the verge of a revolution that is greater than any in the 20th century," says Smit. "There are now composite materials that you can make from plants that are stronger than steel and Kevlar. The implications are phenomenal. Every country in the world could have access to advanced materials created from their own plants."

According to published reports, barely a year after it opened, the thirty-four acre facility has become one of Europe's most popular and celebrated tourist attractions. Meanwhile, Smit is hard at work on his next big project: a campus where business leaders, artists, scientists, engineers, and bureaucrats will commit to spending five days a year sharing their knowledge. "Tithing College is central to my manifesto," Smit explains. "It will attract those who want to imagine a new beginning and contribute to the debate, What does 'great' look like, and how do we get there?"

The Road to Zenlightenment

Journeying down the road of personal and business zenlightenment, it's interesting to contemplate whether we become enlightened first or if the world simply begins to look enlightened to us. A combined theory is that the world becomes enlightened to accommodate a new "enlightened" being. Just as the Buddha, we begin to attract others who are also on the path. They are brought to us in many different ways. Some have called it synchronicity, divine intervention or fate, and I have called it purposeful alignment.

I believe we are entering an era of zenlightened capitalism where the bottom line is only a secondary reason to be in business. Thus we begin to meet other fellow zenlightened entrepreneurs who are on the journey of discovering that the way we do business is the way we conduct our lives, and the way we conduct our lives is much like the Eightfold Buddha principles we've been talking about.

Having met a number of these "zenlightened entrepreneurs" I can tell you that they are totally at peace and at one with the universe. These same individuals run highly successful companies. They say that when their spiritual life is in balance, their business life just seems to flow, not without work, but it flows with ease rather than effort, and they make the right decisions based on "right action" occurring in their lives!

Buddha says:
"The moment we are enlightened within, we go beyond the voidness of a world confronting us."

The Enlightened Ones

What are enlightened people like? Well, some are men and some are women. You might find them in a monastery or a suburban home, in the forest or in a small country town.

It is true that there are not many of them, but there are a lot more than people usually think. It is not that enlightenment is inherently difficult; the sad truth is that most people cannot be bothered to pull themselves out of the bog of ignorance and craving.

Ven. S. Dhammika, in his writings based on the original Buddhist Scriptures, says:

> *"At first you wouldn't notice the enlightened person in a crowd because he's rather quiet and retiring. But when things started to get heated, that's when he'd stand out. When everyone else was enflamed by rage, he'd still be full of love. When others were in turmoil because of some crises, he'd be as calm as he was be-*

fore. In others a mad scramble to get as much as possible, he'd be the one over in the corner with the content expression on his face.

He walks smoothly over the rough; he's steady amid the shaking. It's not that he wants to make a point of being different, rather it's because freedom from desire has made him completely self-contained. But strangely, although others can't move him, his calm presence moves them.

His gentle reasoned words unite those at odds and bring even closer together those already united. The afflicted, the frightened, and the worried feel better after they have talked with him. Wild animals sense the kindness in the enlightened one's heart and are not afraid of him. Even the place where he dwells, be it village, forest, hill or vale, seems more beautiful simply because he is there."

That we have reached the last few pages of this book reminds us of the impermanence of our lives. How quickly the years pass and how soon we will arrive at our final day. The Dalai Lama wrote in his last few pages of *Ethics for the New Millennium:*

"Within less than fifty years, I, Tenzin Gyatso, the Buddhist monk, will be no more than a memory. Indeed, it is doubtful whether a single person reading these words will be alive a century from now.

Time passes uninhindered. When we make mistakes, we cannot turn the clock back and try again. All we can do is use the present well. Therefore, if when our final day comes we are able to look back and see that we have lived full, productive, and meaningful lives that will at least be of some comfort. If we cannot, we may be very sad. Both of which we experience is up to us."

How appropriate that we end this book with the writings of His Holiness the Dalai Lama. We have talked many times about gurus and teachers. The Dalai Lama represents to all whom his life has touched, the one individual on this planet that exemplifies the essence of hope. As we grow to understand ourselves through the guidance of his teachings and others like him, it is important to know that for many of us this is new territory, and like anything untried, the journey must continue. Now that we have tasted the water, we must drink the whole bottle.

Like you, I have been thirsting for answers in search of my soul and the true reasons. This year I took a giant leap of faith and started to examine my inner self very closely. At first, I didn't like what I saw, but as I continued to look deeper and began to take responsibility I was able to right the ship, and have succeeded in at least making the effort to get things right with those people who have been a part of my life for some time.

The Dalai Lama says:

> *"The best way to ensure that when we approach death we do so without remorse is to ensure that in the present moment we conduct ourselves responsibly and with compassion for others."*

> *Actually, this is in our own interest, and not just because it will benefit us in the future. As we have seen, compassion is one of the principal things that make our lives meaningful. It is the source of all lasting happiness and joy. And it is the foundation of a good heart, the heart of one who acts out of a desire to help others.*

> *Through kindness, through affection, through truth and justice toward all others, we ensure our own benefit. This is not a matter for complicated theorizing. It is a matter of common sense. There is no denying that consideration of others is worthwhile. There is no denying that our happiness is inextricably bound up with the happiness of others. There is no denying that if society suffers, we ourselves suffer. Nor is there any denying that the more our*

hearts and minds are afflicted with ill will, the more miserable we become. Thus we can reject everything else: religion, ideology, all received wisdom. But we cannot escape the necessity of love and compassion."

This then is my true religion, my simple faith. I am Jewish but in many ways I choose not to be in a synagogue to be spiritual. You may be Hindu, Muslim or Christian and feel the same need not to be in a temple, mosque or church to experience true spirituality.

The world at this point does not need complicated philosophy, strict doctrines, or rigid dogma. If we look to our heart we need to look no further to find ourselves. Our heart is our mind, our temple. Throughout this entire book, the one ringing theme appears to be compassion. Why? Because ultimately if we love and respect others for their rights and dignity without judgment of who they are, ultimately this will be all we need to survive as a living community. As long as these principles are applied to our daily personal and business life and we teach our children the same, it will not matter what's gone on before. What we have been taught by others, whether we believe in Buddha or God, or are atheists, as long as we have compassion for others and live our lives with restraint out of a moral sense of responsibility, each one of us will be happy.

The Dalai Lama has appealed to us to

"Relinquish our envy, let go your desire to triumph over others. Instead, try to benefit them. With kindness, with courage, and confident that in so doing you are sure to meet with success, welcome others with a smile. Be straightforward. And try to be impartial. Treat everyone as if they were a close friend."

If it is not in your heart for whatever reason to be of help to others, at least try to avoid harming any living creature. We must consider ourselves visitors on this planet. Imagine that you were in outer space and you viewed the world through a telescope. The world yet it is so beautiful. So much like a tourist on vacation in a strange but beautiful place, you would not think for a moment of harming your hosts while you were staying there. Nothing could be gained.

So consider your time on earth a vacation, relax and enjoy yourself and in the midst of your enjoyment take a moment to try to help those who are not so fortunate, those who are downtrodden, and those who for whatever reason cannot help themselves. Too often, we are all guilty, myself included, of turning away from the street people because their appearance is disturbing, with their ragged clothes, their unshaven faces and their physical and mental condition. It is a challenge to not think of yourself as better than them, and yet we are all just two pay cheques away from being in the same condition. Try to not think of them as inferior to yourself, even the humblest beggar. The reality is that when we die we will all look the same in the coffin.

The Dalai Lama has served as an inspiration to us all throughout the book. I quote him regularly because he is one of my heroes. With that said, he is still a human being, just like you and I. The Dalai Lama represents to me the sum total of what the end of this journey towards enlightenment might look like. Peace, serenity, and bliss; no more struggles, no anger, just a flow – a total alignment with purpose and passion.

I wrote this book thinking I could find myself in the process. What I discovered was that the real Allan Holender has always existed, he just needed to appreciate the fact that for this lifetime his mission was to seek and learn so he could help others to ultimately discover who they really are. The truth is we are all the same, and for that reason, we don't need to look very far to find our fellow traveler through this life journey towards enlightenment or nirvana, he or she is right next to us.

I offer you this short prayer, in the hope that it will give you great inspiration as you continue your own personal journey towards zenlightenment.

May I become at all times, both now and forever
    A protector for those without protection
A guide for those who have lost their way
    A ship for those with oceans to cross
A bridge for those with rivers to cross
    A sanctuary for those in danger
    A lamp for those without light
A place of refuge for those who lack shelter
    And a servant to all in need

Namaste

The Constant Zentrepreneur

The Journey Continues at Zentrepreneurism.com

I invite all fellow zentrepreneurs to join me as we continue our lifelong journey of discovery and zenlightenment at

www.zentrepreneurism.com

This website offers a community for like-minded people to meet, collaborate, exchange ideas, share stories, connect, mastermind, and learn more from each other about the new world of Zentrepreneurism. We have established the world's first virtual Centre for Zentrepreneurism. The Z Centre operates from a cyber hub that enables us to connect with each and every one of us, worldwide, that reads the book and wants to keep on zenning!

After you have read the book go to www.zentreprenuerism.com to sign up for our quarterly newsletter, *"The Zen Messenger"* or the monthly *"ZenBiz_ Buzz"*, or both! Just click on the Media icon. It's free! You can also have access to my zenful musings from the past three years since *Zentreprenuerism* gave birth.

At Zentrepreneurism.com you can register for Zentreats, Tele-Summits, Zen Mentoring and Zen Executive Coaching. Coming soon: Webinars, a weekly podcast, and Z-TV. Should you be inspired by this book and its message, I would be honoured to speak at your company, organization, conference or workshop. For a complete outline of topics please go to the Speaking page on the website.

And finally, I would love to hear from you as you begin or continue your journey. You can e-mail me at **allan@zentrepreneurism. com.** Until then, just keep zenning!

Acknowledgments

During the course of research and writing any book an author calls upon the wisdom of others to help clarify his or her own thoughts and beliefs. To that extent, I have quoted many individuals whom I would describe as being in "purposeful alignment" with my journey. It might be said that they are fellow travelers. I would like to recognize the contributions of these individuals, many of whom I have never met. I hope our paths will cross once this book is published. They are listed below in alphabetical order-and if by chance I have left some out, it was unintentional; please accept my sincere apologies.

Abrahamson, Vicki – *The Future Ain't What it Used To Be*, Riverhead Trade; 1999

Bakan, Joel – *The Corporation*, Penguin Books; 2004

Bermudes, Peter – Director of Promotions, Wisdom Publications

Block, Sheri – Writer, *Calgary Herald*; July 29, 2005

Bornstein, David – *How to Change the World: Social Entrepreneurs and the Power of New Ideas*, Oxford University Press; 2004

Boschee, Jerr – National Centre for Social Entrepreneurism

Bogle, John. C – *The Battle for the Soul of Capitalism*, Yale University Press; 2005

Brahm, Ajahn – *Who Ordered this Truckload of Dung – Inspiring Stories for Welcoming Life's Difficulties*, Wisdom Publications; 2005

Brewer, Lynn – *Confessions of an Enron Executive*, Author House; 2004

Brieger, Peter – Writer, *Ottawa Citizen*; August 19, 2005

Canabou, Christine – Writer, *Fast Company*

Cheriton, David – Stanford University

Chopra, Deepak – *Seven Laws of Spiritual Success*, Broadman & Holman; 2002

Cloninger, Robert – *Feeling Good: The Science of Well Being*, Oxford University Press; 2004

Coleman, James – Sociologist

Deutschmann, Alan – Writer, *Fast Company*

Dhammika, Ven. S – Reflections

The Dalai Lama – *An Open Heart*, Time Warner; 2001

East, Nina – *Distinctions of Enlightened Leaders*

Farges, Yves – Founder/CEO Qualifirst Foods

Field, Dr. Lloyd – CEO, Performance House Ltd.

Fitzpatrick, Robert L. – *False Profits: Spiritual Deliverance from Multi-Level Marketing*, Herald Press; 1997, and special thanks for contributing chapter 6.

Gentile, Mary – Aspen Institute

Geshe, Michael Rochet – *The Diamond Cutter – The Buddha on Managing Your Business and Your Life*, Doubleday, 2003

Gold, Stuart Avery – *Dragon Spirit: How to Self-Market Your Dream – A Zentrepreneur's Guide*, Newmarket Press, 2003

Goldsmith, Marshall – Executive Coach

Hamer, Dean – *The God Gene: How Faith is Hardwired into our Genes*, Doubleday; 2004

Hammonds, Keith – Writer, *Fast Company*

Hare, Robert Dr. – University of British Columbia (Department of Psychology)

Hawken, Paul – *Natural Capitalism: Creating the Next Industrial Revolution*, Back Bay Books; 2000

Huffington, Arianna – *Pigs at the Trough: How Corporate Greed and Political Corruption are Undermining America*, Crown; 2003

Johnson, Scott – *Global Environment & Safety Actions*

Karger, Howard – *Shortchanged: Life and Debt in the Fringe Economy*, Berrett-Koehler; 2005

Khosa, Veronica – Ashoka Fellow

Kirkey, Sharon – Writer, CanWest Services; Nov. 14, 2005

Kurzwell, Roy – Inventor, Futurist

Kwon, Beth – Writer, *Fortune Small Business*

Kwong, Laura – Zentrepreneur

Lash, Jonathan – World Resources Institute

Levins, Amory – Co-Author *Natural Capitalism* (see Paul Hawken)

Lovins, Hunter – Co-Author *Natural Capitalism* (see Paul Hawken)

Lesser, Marc – *Z.B.A.: Zen of Business Administration – How Zen Practice Can Transform Your Work and Your Life*, New World Library; 2005

Lewis, Charles – Founder, Centre for Public Integrity

Lorri, John Daido – Author, Artist

Lynch, Peter – *Corporate Social Investing: New Strategies for Giving (and Getting) Corporate Contributions*, Berrett-Koehler, 1998

Mangoven, Bart – *Shareholder Activism: Battlefield of the Future*

Mark, Ellen – Writer, *Fast Company*

Meehan, Mary – Co-Author, *The Future Ain't What it Used to Be*

Newell, Carol – Social Entrepreneur

Newman, Paul – Corporate Social Investing

Novak, Philip – *Buddhism – A Concise Introduction*, Harper; 2003

Palast, Greg – *The Best Democracy Money Can Buy: The Truth About Corporate Cons, Globalization, and High-Finance Fraudsters* Plume; 2003

Pink, Daniel – Author

Read, Nicholas – Writer, *The Vancouver Sun*; August 19, 2005

Reed Business Information Services

Reingold, Jennifer – Writer, *Fast Company*

Richmond, Lewis – *Work as Spiritual Practice: A Practical Buddhist Approach to Inner Growth and Satisfaction on the job*, Broadway Books; 2000

Rubin, Harriet – Writer, *Fast Company*; October 2000

Rohn, Jim – Motivational Speaker

Rubin, Ron – Co-Author *The Dragon Spirit* (see Stuart Gold)

Samuel, Larry – Co-Author *The Future Ain't What it Used to Be*

Schaffer, Jim – "Buddha Talks Business," *Expert Magazine*; January 2004

Silberman, Robert – CEO, Strayer University

Smith, Huston – Co-Author, *Buddhism: A Concise Introduction* (see Philip Novak)

Spitzer, Eliot – New York Attorney General

Stephens, Arran – Buddha Buddy, Founder/CEO, Nature's Path Foods

Stewart, Bruce – Speaker, author, consultant

Strickland, Bill –Social Entrepreneur

Sumedo, Ajahn – *The Mind and the Way: Buddhist Reflections on Life*, Wisdom Publications; 1996

Sweeney, Bob – Buddhist Practitioner

Taylor, Kate – Writer, *The Seattle Times*; 2005

Tedesco, Teresa – Writer, *The Ottawa Citizen*; August 19, 2005

Templeton, David – Author, *American Buddhist*

Tischler, Linda – Writer, *Fast Company*; September, 2005

Thurman, Robert – Columbia University (Professor Buddhist Studies)

Tracy, Pat – Founder/CEO Dot Foods

Underwood, Ryan – Writer, *Fast Company*

Useem, Jerry – Writer, *Fortune Magazine*

Weeden, Curt – *Corporate Social Investing* (see Peter Lynch)

Wray, William – *Sayings of the Buddha: Reflections for Every Day, Arcturus*; 2004

Zacharias, Yvonne – Writer, *The Vancouver Sun*; September 24, 2005

About the Author

As a leadership and team-building trainer, Allan Holender has developed and delivered programs to colleges, universities, hospitals and the corporate world. He has mentored entrepreneurs, CEOs, and senior management from some of North America's top-ranked companies. He is also a popular media personality and commentator in Canada and the United States, having hosted a nationally syndicated business radio show on the Talk America Radio Network. As a speaker he has addressed thousands across Canada and the U. S., and captured a worldwide audience through his web-related media appearances.

Allan gained his knowledge through first-hand experience as a business owner, "serial" entrepreneur, CEO, manager, leadership expert, teacher, writer, and broadcaster. He delivers his life lessons with both passion and humor—helping others to create balance between the important elements of one's life. Born in Edmonton, Alberta, Allan holds a bachelor of arts in Sociology from the University of Montana. He went on to graduate school and shortly thereafter began a long career with the Big Brothers organization. Later he assumed senior administrative positions in advancement with the Universities of British Columbia and Alberta. Allan is a pioneer in the fund development industry, having founded two professional associations.

Allan is available for speaking engagements, radio shows, and professional consultations. He can be contacted through email at **allan@zentrepreneurism.com.**